Graeme Leak is an acc-
laimed performer, composer
and instrument maker, with
a background in percussion
and drumming. Since com-
pleting studies at the
Sydney Conservatorium of
Music (1978) and in New
York (1985), he has made an
original and distinguished
contribution to Australian
music.

Graeme's diverse activit-
ies include a decade with the legendary Flederman
Ensemble (which championed new Australian music
throughout the 1980s), regular appearances in
Melbourne's ASTRA concerts, seasons at The Last Laugh
(a comedy-cabaret venue), solo recitals across Australia,
the US and Europe, plus many innovative projects in
music-theatre, dance and improvised music.

Parallel to his local and international performing
career, Graeme has held teaching positions at the
Queensland Conservatorium, the Canberra School of
Music, the Sydney Conservatorium and La Trobe
University. He regularly conducts public music
workshops and acts as music director for large-scale
events. Graeme is currently institutionally unattached.

The string can: An easily-constructed, home-made instrument (see page 138). (Photographer: Graeme Leak.)

GRAEME LEAK

PERFORMANCE MAKING

A
manual
for
music
workshops

Currency Press,
Sydney

First published in 2003 by Currency Press.

Currency Press Pty Ltd
PO Box 2287, Strawberry Hills NSW 2012 Australia
enquiries@currency.com.au
www.currency.com.au

National Library of Australia—Cataloguing-in-publication Data
Leak, Graeme.
       Performance making: a manual for music workshops.
       ISBN 0 86819 673 8.
       1. Music—Performance—Instruction and study. I. Title.
       781.43

Cover design by Kate Florance, Currency Press, using a photo of
Kevin Man performing as part of the Percussion Maintenance
Team at the Queensland Biennial Festival of Music in 1999.
(Photographer: Graeme Leak.)

Photograph of Graeme Leak on page i reproduced courtesy of the
Mercury.

Set in Californian FB 10/13.5.

Printed by Ligare Book Printer, Riverwood.

CONTENTS

PART TWO: WORKSHOP TECHNIQUES

Graeme Leak in a performance-making workshop at NSW
Government House in 2000. (Photographer: Ross Heathcote.)

ACKNOWLEDGMENTS

I would like to thank the many people who have contributed to this work: Richard Vella for his patience, support and encouragement; Meredith Rogers, with whom I shared drama/music classes at La Trobe University (these classes were a joy and an inspiration); the many students and workshop participants whom I've had the pleasure to interact with; my colleagues from La Trobe University's Music Department, which sadly closed in 1999; Kate Florance, my editor at Currency Press, for her remarkable clarity and polish; John Cameron, Neil Kelly, Helen Saniga and Lynne Leak for their invaluable feedback on early drafts; Ros Warby, who was the model for the isolation and stretching photographs; and finally my partner, Caroline, and our children, Alex and Jackson. I am blessed with an understanding and supportive family.

QUOTES

'Music is not just notes on paper.'

I have included quotes from some of my workshop participants. I had gathered the comments during workshops and circulated them amongst participants on an anonymous basis. I wasn't planning to publish them, but they are illuminating and insightful. I thank the authors (whom I have been unable to contact) and vouch that they are real with minor nip and tuck edits.

IDEAS AND OWNERSHIP

This is not an academic text or a theoretical discourse. This is a practical manual gleaned from my own experiences as a teacher and performer. I have always tended to learn by doing.

There are many ideas in this book that I can't claim as my own. Some of the exercises, for example, I have picked up along the way, perhaps in Meredith's classes or in workshops I have attended. I have included my versions of these exercises in the context of music making. Similarly, I don't claim to be a movement expert, but I have found the stretches outlined in these pages to be invaluable in the performance-making context.

I owe a debt to R. Murray Schafer's *Ear Cleaning* (BMI Canada 1967); Keith Johnstone's *Impro* (Faber & Faber Ltd 1979); and Richard Vella's *Musical Environments* (Currency Press 2000). I still refer to a few of my favourite drum books: Pete Magadini's *The Musician's Guide to Polyrhythms* (Drum Center Books 1996); George Lawrence Stone's *Stick Control* (George B. Stone & Sons, Inc. 1935); and Louis Bellson's *Modern Reading Texts in 4/4* (Belwin c 1963). And I refer regularly to a boxed set of *Oblique Strategy* cards by Brian Eno and Peter Schmidt (Opal Ltd 1975, 1978, 1979). These cards are great creative tools—pulled at random—and I recommend them as a source of inspiration when your own is waning.

DISCLAIMER

The publisher and the author accept no responsibility for any injuries sustained by anyone attempting any of the exercises described in this book. People who have an injury, a medical condition or who are unfit should seek medical advice before undertaking these exercises.

INTRODUCTION

For many years I have worked as a workshop leader, directing people in sessions that result in the performance of a work created by the group.

I have encountered people frightened to improvise, fearful of performance and terrified of being 'judged'.

By adapting a process usually associated with drama called performance making, I have found ways to help break down fears and inhibitions, and to create exciting music performances.

Many of the games and exercises in this book have been borrowed from the rich traditions of teaching drama and adapted to the context of teaching music. This is because performance making acknowledges that the creation of music is inherently theatrical in gesture (because, after all, as soon as someone begins to make sounds and others are watching and listening, there is music-theatre).

Although performance making focuses on the realm of sound, due to its dramatic context, it also incorporates both physical and visual elements.

WHO THIS BOOK IS FOR

This book is primarily for the leader of a music workshop. It assumes that the leader has:
▶ a basic knowledge, both practical and theoretical, of music and music notation;

▶ some experience in teaching, either one-to-one or to groups.

This book may also be useful in contexts beyond the arts. Its exploration of game-playing, listening, risk-taking and collective creativity can be used to encourage team-building and to enhance communication skills. In particular, the performance-making principles are highly transferable to the areas of improving workplace relations and sport performance (see page 7).

WHO CAN ATTEND PERFORMANCE-MAKING WORKSHOPS?

Anyone! Workshop participants can range from complete beginners to accomplished professionals, from inexperienced non-musicians to professional instrumentalists or singers from any style or tradition, from amateurs wanting to 'get their act together' to performers from other disciplines (actors, dancers and circus performers) wanting to improve their skills in music. All can benefit from learning these performance-making techniques.

HOW TO USE THIS BOOK

This book is designed for workshops teaching musical performance skills through a process of exploration, improvisation and group music making.

The goal of every performance-making workshop session is an in-house group performance, and the ultimate aim of a series of workshops is a final group performance, preferably to an outside audience. This book provides the resources for a leader to run a workshop and to create a performance out of the workshop process.

Part one guides the workshop leader through the process of running a performance-making workshop:

▶ how to inspire performance making using some basic principles;
▶ how to set up a workspace;
▶ how to plan a workshop; and
▶ how to create performances out of the workshop pieces.

Part two outlines the techniques and exercises used during the workshops to:

▶ warm up physically and mentally;
▶ tune into a playful, open and creative state of mind;
▶ learn music skills; and
▶ encourage participants to experience and explore the various elements of music through their bodies.

The workshop techniques can be adapted to the particular context of workshop delivery. If you require a course for high school, university or technical college, there is enough for a single semester course of between ten and fourteen sessions. If you are an independent arts practitioner running classes, you might need a three or four session design. You could also devise a single, one-off session.

You can use the resources in this book to structure course outlines and session plans according to your own requirements and the needs of the particular group you are working with. Sample course outlines are included in appendix one.

See appendix four for a glossary of musical terms.

Overleaf is a diagram of how the book can be used.

HOW TO USE THIS BOOK

PERFORMANCE MAKING PRINCIPLES
- ▶ Nurture creativity   ▶ Maintain focus
- ▶ Don't be judgmental   ▶ Show commitment
- ▶ Let go of fear

SESSION/WORKSHOP PLANNING

WORKSHOP TECHNIQUES

ISOLATION
EXERCISES

STRETCHES
- ▶ Floor
- ▶ Standing

WARM-UPS
- ▶ Listening
- ▶ Moving
- ▶ Making sounds

GAMES
- ▶ Name games
- ▶ Playground games
- ▶ Status games
- ▶ Drama games

MUSIC SKILLS
- ▶ Pulse
- ▶ The note 'A'
- ▶ Tones and semitones
- ▶ Triads

EXERCISES
- ▶ Noise
- ▶ Silence
- ▶ Pulse
- ▶ Metre
- ▶ Rhythm
- ▶ Tone
- ▶ Melody and harmony
- ▶ Timbre
- ▶ Dynamics
- ▶ Texture
- ▶ Duration

PERFORMANCE TASKS

FEEDBACK SESSIONS

PERFORMANCES

PART ONE: RUNNING A WORKSHOP

The Percussion Maintenance Team at the Queensland Biennial Festival of Music in 1999. (Photographer: Graeme Leak.)

CHAPTER 1: WHAT IS PERFORMANCE MAKING?

THE BODY AS THE ULTIMATE INSTRUMENT

Music comes from our bones and our being. The body is the consummate performance instrument for music, dance and drama. Music doesn't come from musical instruments; musical instruments simply amplify and project innate musicianship.

The role of the body is acknowledged in the teaching, theory and practice of dance and drama, yet very little attention is paid to the use of the body in musical performance. Perhaps this is because there is so much focus on the instruments of music and their incumbent techniques and traditions. Musical training tends to favour the learning of technique and repertoire over the important and sometimes more difficult work of nurturing the musical imagination and the musical ear. Technique can be (relatively) easy to teach—it can be codified, graded and examined—yet musical ideas can often be imprisoned by the techniques and structures of various musical genres.

Performance-making techniques concentrate on the body and allow us to tap into a universal form of musical thinking which is not constrained by genre, such as 'classical' or 'blues'. Once we learn to clap in time, sing in tune and dance or move about theatrically, it is possible to create compelling performance pieces, which we can watch with our ears blocked or listen to with our eyes closed. We can also easily transfer these musical skills onto how we play instruments and so enhance the music we produce via the instruments.

HOW TO MAKE MUSIC

To make a piece of music all you need is:
▶ a way to start;
▶ a way to stop;
▶ no fear of silence.
To make music you also need to feel:
▶ confident;
▶ empowered;
▶ responsible.
And to make the piece work as a performance you need to be ready to:
▶ listen;
▶ trust.
These are the basic ingredients for a successful musical performance.

Music skills, like any skills, improve with practice. They can be dramatically improved through performance-making techniques.

PERFORMANCE MAKING

▶ Encompasses making sounds, listening, imagining and challenging ideas.
▶ Emphasises the development of the musical imagination. It aims to fire participants' imagination to the point where it becomes clear which techniques are needed in order to realise their ideas. Technique

becomes a servant to ideas, which is far healthier than ideas being imprisoned by techniques.

▶ Nurtures the musical ear. The group process demands a high level of listening: to others, to yourself and to the whole piece. Participants investigate 'what makes a performance work?' and this develops their listening skills.

▶ Develops an awareness of the musical performing body. The process assumes that the body is the primary instrument, and it uses a lot of clapping, stomping and vocalising to develop musicianship without reference to any particular style. It operates on a universal level, which is transferable to any instrument or voice in any style. By moving the emphasis away from the restrictions and safety of instruments and scores, and by making pieces with movement, pictures and sounds, new possibilities unfold.

▶ Gives responsibility for all elements of the performance to the performers, who become composer–performers. Participants are not told what to perform; this is up to them. They generate all the material for a performance. No pre-existing scores or other musical structures are referred to. Exercises assist participants to release their creative energies and increase their level of confidence and trust in their performances. Performance making is a kind of composition through performance.

▶ Relies on trust, thrives on spontaneity and impulse, and helps develop confidence and self-assurance.

▶ Does not call for a particular skill level from participants. Instead the ability to take risks is crucial, as well as being open-minded.

▶ Can turn perceived weaknesses into strengths— don't hide your weaknesses, explore them and put them on display.

► Allows workshops to be style-free. Conventional training tends to focus on the development of music skills for a particular genre or style (classical, jazz, country, R & B, rock and so on). Performance making both ignores and accepts all styles. It exists outside musical styles so the skills and experiences gained are transferable to and will enrich all styles.

Performance making is about:
► finding connections;
► exploring new territory;
► discovering;
► removing blocks;
► stumbling;
► realising;
► jumping and landing, and not getting hurt.

'People from different backgrounds and with different ideas can join forces and create a really effective performance. We hear about these things happening but it's great when you are actually a part of it.'

CHAPTER 2: PERFORMANCE-MAKING PRINCIPLES

The following principles can be used to inspire the group discussions that become a regular part of performance-making workshops. Generally they centre on belief and fear. As so much about music and performing is connected to belief, it's useful to talk about it. It's also a good way to start with any new group.

(1) NURTURE CREATIVITY

I believe all people are by nature creative, but most people seem to believe that they are not. People are afraid of ideas and lack confidence in their impulses. Creativity is a belief, not a talent, and belief in this creativity is fundamental to performance making. The workshop process builds confidence in using ideas and provides experiences in acting creatively and spontaneously by giving participants:

▶ the necessary tools and workspace;
▶ the power to make something;
▶ the responsibility to make it work.

Performance making can bring about a fundamental change in belief from 'I am not creative and cannot act spontaneously' to 'my ideas are valid and my impulses are worth following'.

A performer becoming creative is like a snail emerging from its shell. When the snail makes its first attempt to leave its shell, the slightest interference can cause it to withdraw. The performer needs to feel confident to emerge from his or her shell, and to risk acting creatively and spontaneously.

Everybody has a right to feel that his or her ideas are important. Workshop leaders should understand and respect this, and allow each member of the group to have her or his voice heard. To make sure that everyone in the group feels secure and confident to speak, the group should consider the issue of being judgmental.

'In the beginning I was aware of a general lack of ideas. But as soon as we picked the energy levels up, by deciding to have fun, ideas began to flow and the piece came into existence.'

'It was a creative, fun time with shared input and ideas from everyone.'

(2) DON'T BE JUDGMENTAL

A major block to creativity and spontaneity is being judgmental.

First, there is the nagging internal voice:

'No, I won't offer that thought, because my ideas are no good.'

'Well, I think it would work better if we did it another way, but they know better than me so I'll keep quiet and go along with it this way.'

'I don't know how she thinks of these things. She's so creative and amazing.'

A primary aim of performance making is to learn to short-circuit that moment of being judgmental about yourself and to ignore that over-critical voice from within. Games are an important part of performance-making workshops, as they help participants to trust their impulses and to be more spontaneous, creative and playful. Another technique used to lessen the likelihood of participants being judgmental is to create short-term performance goals, for example, 'you have five minutes to prepare a performance for the rest of the class, starting now'. The brief preparation period allows participants to trust their impulses and to create exciting and risky work.

Then there are the external voices to contend with—the stated opinions of others. A performance-making group needs to establish some standards about what to say to each other to ensure that a nurturing and positive atmosphere prevails. See the feedback section on page 27.

Finally there is what we imagine others are thinking. In 99 per cent of cases this imagined judgment doesn't materialise in the real world. A performance-making group learns to recognise and eradicate this unnecessary and debilitating fear. You don't need to be anyone other than yourself.

> 'People in our group are not there to judge
> ... but most people are worried about what
> others think.'

(3) LET GO OF FEAR

There is a widespread fear of making music. Many people believe that they can't sing or that they don't have rhythm, so they are afraid to even try.

Performance making assumes that everyone can learn to recognise, use and explore the musical ingredients of low and high, fast and slow, loud and soft, long and short. Experience is a major factor in skill development, and music skills can be developed through exercises exploring these musical concepts. The more experience you have, the more confident you can become with a particular skill. This doesn't mean that you are better than someone with less experience. Within a performance-making group, it is important to ensure that your experience doesn't intimidate others. A workshop leader should aim to ensure that each member benefits from the skills and experiences of other members of the group.

In any group, there will be a range of skill levels; a young child with no musical experience may be alongside professional adult musicians. It is important that participants simply acknowledge where they are at. The workshop atmosphere should be absolutely non-competitive—participants should be aiming for honesty in performance, rather than being fearful of not being 'the best'. The workshop should be an environment where each participant can get experience in the areas they would like to focus on, with the encouragement and support of the others.

> 'My aim is to come out of my shell and join in the discussions, and not be scared of what I have to say.'

The workshop process creates a space for you to experiment and make mistakes. To learn to ride a bike you probably fell off a few times, and without falling off you would never learn to stay on. Performance making is like that—mistakes will be made and accepting this is vital.

'Loud and confident' is a good group motto, even if participants feel they are doing something wrong ... but is there any such thing as 'wrong' in performance?

Theoretically, participants are at the peak of their abilities because they are as old and as wise as they can possibly be.

Provided the conditions of listening, trust and responsibility prevail, then any contribution is valid and can't be considered 'right' or 'wrong'.

> 'We are thinking a lot more about our performance as an entity in space, and its place in relation to the audience. We are addressing some of the issues of performance and becoming more comfortable.'

> 'His performance stood out because he appeared confident: loud and clear.'

> 'Mistakes don't have to be the end of the world.'

(4) MAINTAIN FOCUS

Performance making requires focus. The ability to find focus, stay focused and to shift focus, plus an awareness of the audience's focus, are central to making a performance work.

> 'Today everyone seemed more tuned in to their pieces and the performances reflected this.'

> 'The audience was only distracting if I focused on them, so I shifted my focus to the performance and the audience conversation became a muttered conversation.'

> 'A group needs to have each member on an equal energy level because if they're not, the performance loses an incredible amount of authority.'

> 'Anything can be a performance. It's the attitude, through focus, that makes it work.'

(5) SHOW COMMITMENT

TO THE PROCESS

Group members need to be committed to the performance-making process. Of course they should question, challenge and speak up about how things are developing, but without a fundamental commitment to performance making by each and every member of the group, the process itself can't work.

TO THE MOMENT

One participant in a class put it beautifully:

> 'You can only be 'in' or 'out' of performance mode. If you're 'out' then don't perform. You are not performing if you are in the middle of 'in' and 'out'—you might as well be in the audience.'

A commitment needs to be made to the moment in order for it to become a performance. Traditionally, musicians in rehearsal don't do this—they tend to build towards the actual performance using a different energy in rehearsal and performance.

This is not so in performance making. Everyone is 'in' from the moment they enter the workspace, right from day one.

'A lot ... can be made of listening to what the moment demands and adapting to it.'

TO THE GROUP

Each member needs to commit to the group. This means, in practical terms, allowing others to speak, respecting the abilities and limitations of others, listening at all times and supporting others as they attempt new and possibly confronting situations.

'I don't think we allowed enough room for all the sounds to come through, that we rushed it a bit and sort of tried to get our individual moments of glory.'

'Individuals need to surrender their desire to control a group in order for the group to function as a whole.'

'I've learnt that in order for a group of people to work together on a project, each person must have patience and respect for others in the group.'

CHAPTER 3: SETTING UP A WORKSPACE

THE IDEAL WORKSPACE

The workspace for performance making is preferably a large open space with a wooden floor. It should have enough ceiling height to play a ball game comfortably, plenty of natural light and access to fresh air. It should be possible to cool the space in summer and warm it in winter, and its acoustics should respond well to voices, body percussion and musical instruments. It should be isolated from other areas so as not to disturb anyone and to promote a sense of privacy and safety. It should not be subject to aural invasion from air-conditioners, power tools or traffic. It should be possible to transform it into a performance space by blacking out the windows (with thick curtains) and setting up a few theatre lamps and possibly a sound system.

There should be a supply of staging and rostra in a storeroom nearby, as well as a variety of chairs, music stands and a collection of junk and found percussion instruments.

There should be some side spaces suitable for rehearsing in small groups, and these should be isolated enough to enable each group to focus.

A good quality CD/tape playback system is essential, with a recording facility to enable easy and good quality audio recording of pieces as they develop. It's amazing how the group will respond to hearing their own work even one week after it was made—with the advantage of some distance and objectivity, the group is usually surprised at how good they sound on tape or CD. There should be a piano in the main space ... and a cafe, toilets and parking not too far away.

FALLBACK OPTIONS (FOR THOSE WHO DON'T LIVE IN AN IDEAL WORLD)

If there are no side rooms, it's better to have carpet in the big space. That way the smaller groups can work independently in the extreme corners (but this can still get noisy). If there is not enough ceiling height, an adjacent outdoor space can be used for games and the more active warm-ups. You really do need a supply of natural light and fresh air, and a degree of sound isolation. (It's difficult to get any real work done under fluorescent lights in an airless room listening to the neighbours or air-conditioners humming.)

A portable CD/tape player is a temporary solution but there is no substitute for quality audio equipment.

Other elements (blackout materials, rostra and percussion instruments) can be improvised. Lighting can consist of simple clamp or desk lamps—I've even put overhead projectors to good use as light sources (they work well with transparencies, bubble wrap or cellophane). In another performance we used battery torches to good effect.

CHAPTER 4: PLANNING A WORKSHOP

PLANNING A COURSE

At the heart of the performance-making method is a set of exercises that focus on specific musical elements:

▶ noise;
▶ silence;
▶ pulse;
▶ metre;
▶ rhythm;
▶ tone;
▶ melody and harmony;
▶ timbre;
▶ dynamics;
▶ texture;
▶ duration.

These become themes for individual sessions and can also be used in planning the structure of the course.

A semester course of ten to twelve sessions could focus on each element in turn, with a final performance that seeks to display the results of the group's exploratory work. A single session could focus on a single element or give a less-detailed introduction to several.

Planning the course calls for the skills and backgrounds of participants to be taken into account. For example, if you are working mostly with vocalists and melody instrument players they might respond best to sessions centred on pitch, melody and harmony. A mixed group of skilled and unskilled participants could find common ground in areas such as texture, pulse, noise and silence. It is important to respond to the needs of the group and organise the session materials in such a way that all participants are actively engaged and enjoying the sessions.

See appendix one for one-, three- and ten-session course plans. I've found it best to plan courses 'on the fly' and in response to the outcomes of the previous session. For this reason, the ten-session course plan has some options to choose from after session six. In fact, sessions eight and nine may well be devoted to just detailing and running the final performance.

The session plans are included as a guide only. Sessions should be tailored to your group and its progress. Sometimes it's best to abandon all plans and run with unexpected developments in the work at the time.

PLANNING A SESSION

Here is a basic plan for each session:

▶ A ritual to start. Have some sort of ritual at the start of the session—perhaps you could tidy the space, put your bags away and take your shoes off, or participants might arrive and quietly do some individual stretching until everyone is present and the session starts.

▶ Stretches and warm-ups. Try stretching and floor work followed by some standing and moving exercises. If you run a series of classes then soon this part of the class can look after itself.

▶ Games. Play some games to release energy and laughter, and to pick up the pace.

▶ Elemental exercises. These form the core of the group work. Work with the whole group as you introduce concepts and practise the skills using exercises.

▶ Discussions are ongoing and occur throughout the process. Refer to performance-making principles such as letting go of fear in relation to the work being done, and feed these discussions back into the performances.

▶ Set a performance task. Split the group up into smaller groups and ask each to prepare a response to the exercise material just workshopped. While they are in separate areas working, visit each group and assist where necessary.

▶ Perform to each other. Reconvene the class to watch and listen to each performance.

▶ Conduct a feedback session. Feedback sessions are forums to discuss a range of issues related to the work just done and the planned direction the work might take. The leader facilitates and guides the process, encouraging each participant to claim ownership, to take responsibility and to make contributions in discussions. Round out the session by setting work for the next meeting.

PLANNING THE FIRST SESSION

The first session is introductory by nature, but make sure it does not become a talkfest with no action—every session should include some performances at the end. Assuming a two-hour duration, the first session could follow this plan:

WARM-UP

Send the clap around (page 68).	3 minutes
Send the sound around (page 68).	3 minutes

GAME

Play the ball name game (page 70).   5 minutes
Play the barrier name game (page 71).   5 minutes

DISCUSS

Hand out a course structure and discuss
the main ideas, expectations, ground rules
and questions.   20 minutes

EXERCISES

Working with the whole group, focus on pulse:
(page 89)   20 minutes
▶ independent pulse;
▶ unified pulse;
▶ from slow to fast;
▶ grouped in twos, threes, fours and fives (metre).

PERFORMANCE TASK

In groups of three to five, explore the following task.
▶ 'Today's task is to make a piece that goes from
   independent to unified pulse. It has variation in
   speed (some slow, some medium and some fast bits)
   and a variety of metres (at least three). Use clapping,
   stomping and vocal sounds only.'   4 minutes
Allocate the groups before the break.

BREAK   15 minutes

SMALL GROUP REHEARSALS

Visit each group a few times to monitor
   progress.   15 minutes

PERFORMANCES

Reconvene to listen to each performance.   15 minutes

FEEDBACK

Ask for responses from the performers
   and the audience.   15 minutes

Use names as often as possible, and make an effort to learn all names in the first session.

Usually the plan contains more material than you actually get through. It's worth keeping notes on this and modifying your expectations and plans.

SELECTING THE GROUP

Accommodating a range of skills and experience levels in one group can be difficult. If you have the luxury of running several groups in parallel then it would be useful to group them according to their relative skill base. It is also useful to run an introductory two or three hour session as the first session in your planned series. It will become clear very quickly who is going to respond to the workshops and benefit from the experience. This will allow some group members to say 'I don't think this is for me' and to decide not to participate. If anyone is openly sceptical, cynical or suspicious it's probably not for them, and it's not for the group either. People with these attitudes are like ice in the creative stockpot—you'll have to wait for them to thaw before they can become part of the group, so it may be easier to just give them an opportunity to opt out.

Ideally the group shouldn't be larger than fifteen. Between ten and fifteen is a good size—less than ten can work too, but the possibilities for varying the combinations in smaller groups are a bit restricted. More than fifteen can also work, but you will need to consider the available space. It is important to be able to split the larger group into smaller work parties regularly. And remember, if it is an odd-numbered group then you'll be jumping every time you work in pairs!

USING THE PERFORMANCE-MAKING PRINCIPLES

The principles outlined above underpin all of the action in the workspace. They should be referred to continually in the planning, execution and feedback phases of performance making. The more often they are reinforced and reintroduced, the better. For example:

(1) TO ADDRESS BELIEFS AND FEARS REGARDING MUSICAL ABILITY

Discuss:

▶ Skills improve with experience;
▶ Experience breeds confidence;
▶ Lack of experience is not equal to lack of ability.

(2) TO ACCOMMODATE A RANGE OF SKILL LEVELS IN ONE GROUP

Discuss:

▶ The experience of one shouldn't intimidate another—instead, it can inspire and motivate;
▶ It's not a competition;
▶ How can we establish a nurturing and supportive environment?

(3) TO SHORT-CIRCUIT BEING JUDGMENTAL (TO SILENCE THE OVER-CRITICAL INNER VOICE)

▶ Use clear instructions with a narrow focus. If the instruction says 'play', boundless possibilities can overwhelm participants. If the instruction has a specific and narrow focus, such as 'play a note that starts loud and becomes soft' the task seems easy. Decisions about which note, how long, the speed from loud to soft etc. can be made spontaneously.
▶ Use lots of short-term goals. Short-term performance tasks are the staple activity. Why make one piece when you can make fifty and choose the best one?

► Say 'yes' whenever an offer comes along from a participant and try it in action immediately. Keep talking to a minimum and action to a maximum.

(4) USE 'EXTERNAL VOICES' TO ADVANTAGE
► Ensure that everyone understands the importance of giving and receiving feedback. Establish a meaningful feedback loop that considers what to say to each other with a focus on specifics. This will quickly get rid of any 'imagined judgment'.

SETTING WORKSHOP GOALS
SHORT-TERM GOALS
Set regular short-term goals—'you have five minutes to prepare a performance, starting now'—to motivate and propel the action. The lack of time to prepare makes it essential to suspend being judgmental about ideas, and allows for a greater level of spontaneity.

MEDIUM-TERM GOALS
If you are running a longer course it's a good idea to introduce and discuss a course outline in the first session that makes medium-term goals clear from the start. An example of a medium-term goal might be a 'showing' to friends and families at a mid-point in the course. Another medium-term goal might be to make certain decisions by a certain date. For example, where will the performance take place? Who is taking care of publicity, the program, costumes, sets and sound design?

A midpoint review of the material produced so far and some broad decisions about the overview or shape of the final piece is recommended. Make sure that everyone understands that the material created in the class will be the material for the final performance. Often groups panic when you start talking about the performance and start dreaming up unrelated material.

Keep the focus on the material taking form in the classes, and take charge if it starts to go awry.

THE PERFORMANCE

A public performance is the ultimate goal of the sessions. The date for this should be set from the outset. The choice of venue might be left to the group, or you might already have it booked. Duration can be anywhere from 20 minutes to an hour—it depends on the context of the performance.

Is it possible to run sessions that don't lead to a performance? No. The performance is essential as the ultimate goal. If you can only run one or two sessions, these can result in an in-house performance where half the group watches as the other half performs, then they can swap. Alternatively a performance involving everyone can be videotaped so that all can view and discuss it.

> 'Opportunities and ideas are all around us really. All we need to do is be open and receptive to them.'

STAYING ON SCHEDULE

It is important to be disciplined in keeping to the schedule. The sessions should always start on time so if people are late, they will be entering a space where work is well under way. This calls for the leader to arrive well before the first person does and to be prepared for the class.

Plan the estimated time for each activity and move things on if they get bogged down. Don't hesitate to abandon the plan if it's not working! If the energy lags or the focus is lost, try alternative ideas or improvise new plans.

SETTING PERFORMANCE TASKS

Performance tasks are instructions that need to be carefully considered and very clear. Use simple and direct language. Clarify any questions before breaking the group into work parties. Some themes that are useful:

FROM/TO

'Make a piece which goes from ". . ." to ". . ." .' For example, if the group has been exploring timbre (tone, colour), the instruction could be to make a piece about a change in sound colour from 'dark' to 'light'. Then the question of how you get from one state to another can be explored. Is it sudden, or slow? Does everyone change at the same time? Do some change in the reverse direction? This universally adaptable instruction can apply from 'noise' to 'silence', from 'high' to 'low' and so on.

SUMMARISE, COMBINE AND RESOLVE

After working with specific elemental exercises, ask the groups to summarise, combine and resolve these into a coherent piece that refers directly to the material just explored, with variations.

MAPPING

Use the spatial and drama games as musical maps and play them with instruments/voices. For example, perform the directed walking exercises where the group is moving through the space in straight lines, curvy lines, jagged lines and parallel lines at a fast pace, slow pace, with stops and so on; then ask the group to transfer this to instruments. Sitting or standing in one place playing sounds, they can refer to an imaginary shape and contour that they have just physically experienced.

USE CHANCE-COMPOSITION METHODS

Try out the chance-composition methods of the influential American composer, John Cage (1912–1992). Cage did some pioneering work in interrogating the processes of composing and performing music, and this lead him to explore the concept of randomness as a compositional technique. After Cage had developed a new method for musical composition and had utilised it to create new works, he would often abandon it and try something new; he never allowed the methods and structures (of his own making) to become prisons.

Some examples of Cage's chance-composition methods are:

▶ Determine parameters such as duration, colour, dynamics etc. by tossing coins. You can decide how to implement this idea—Cage worked with the *I Ching* (also known as the *Book of Changes*, this is an ancient Chinese book of wisdom which may be consulted using the tossing of coins).

▶ Devise charts and graphs containing details of any number of musical structures and/or parameters, and determine performances by choosing these randomly. Once again, Cage used to consult the *I Ching* to choose gestures related to, for example, duration and dynamics.

▶ Randomly cut up existing scores, texts and instruction sets into small pieces and have players choose them out of a hat during a performance or as part of a rehearsal.

▶ Use radios as musical instruments, tuning in to both the stations and the sound in between the stations.

▶ Formulate rules about determining parameters using the throwing of dice, then throw the dice to determine the parameters.

I strongly recommend that you experiment with Cage's chance-composition methods. See the composer's scores and writings, available in larger music shops and in some university libraries (La Trobe University has an extensive collection). For further reading, see *The Music of John Cage* by James Pritchett (Cambridge University Press 1993).

USE TIME AS STRUCTURE

'Make a four minute piece. In the first 30 seconds try "blah", in the next 90 seconds, try "blah" and so on.'

See appendix one for an extensive collection of performance tasks.

The interesting thing is the amazing diversity of responses you get from presenting the same instruction to different people. Paradoxically, it seems that when the instruction is narrower and more prescriptive, the performances are more inventive, exploratory and creative.

CHOOSING SUBGROUPS

When it is time to break into smaller groups, keep watch on the dynamics of different groupings and try different combinations. Some participants take a more enthusiastic and active role, some are committed but more passive, while others can be quite blocking, negative and counter-productive (perhaps without realising it). And people move between these states all the time—sometimes in the one session a person is all three of the above.

These massive generalisations obviously don't cover the huge complexities of group dynamics but I have found it helpful to identify active, passive and counter-productive personalities when it comes to splitting up classes into smaller groups.

Active people translate their ideas quickly into actions and follow through on discussed agreements. If she says, 'I'll design the flier', she'll turn up with a draft design at the next session. When working in a group, active people want to do rather than talk about doing.

Passive people participate willingly but tend not to take the initiative, preferring to let others direct the discussion or work session. This can cause problems when their lack of response is misinterpreted. Ms Active might be thinking, 'I think I'm leading this too much, but he's not saying anything so he must be happy' whereas Mr Passive is really thinking, 'I'm really unhappy with the way she takes over but I'm not going to say anything—I'll just go along with it'.

Counter-productive people do things that slow the process, like complaining about the task without offering a solution to the problems, or splitting the focus by performing irrelevant material while the group is trying to work, or simply not turning up to sessions.

The great thing about performance making is that it can help people understand how their actions have an effect on others—if they let their group down, the others in the group usually tell them about it.

An effective subgroup should have a mix of these kinds of people rather than a predominance of any one type. Active members become key players in a sense and need to be distributed evenly throughout the subgroups.

▶ Keep an eye on which combinations spark and which ones don't.

▶ Take notes and plan the groupings for each session.

▶ If the group seems to be floundering during the session, switch people around or step in and help things along.

THE FEEDBACK LOOP

What is the role and function of critical feedback? If you play something for a group, it's really good to discover what they were thinking about during your performance. If you play to ten people or one thousand people you will get as many unique responses to your performance. Feedback can be a potent force in the development of a performer.

'I began to feel how the idea of an audience could positively affect a performer. I felt that there was an energy that could be gained from the relationship and that there was no real need for fear.'

'It was very rewarding just to get other people's comments and to see that we had had an effect on people.'

Before the groups perform to each other, ask the performers to consider:
▶ Where do you want the audience (that is, those not performing)?
▶ How are you going to start and stop?
▶ Where is the entrance from?
▶ Who cues the start?
▶ Is there enough light to see everyone in the group?
▶ Are there any sight line problems for the audience?

Ask the audience to consider or note down the following:

PERFORMANCE
▶ What was each performer trying to do?
▶ How well has he or she done it?
▶ Was the whole group really focused and 'in' the performance throughout?
▶ If not, who was and who wasn't? Was there a turning point?
▶ Which parts of the piece really worked? Why?

- ▶ Which parts of the piece didn't work? Why?
- ▶ Were there aspects of this performance that could be further developed and explored?
- ▶ Can you imagine transferring this subgroup performance to a whole group performance?

PRACTICALITIES
- ▶ What was the entrance and exit like?
- ▶ How was the positioning of the audience?
- ▶ Were there any sight line problems? For example, did a music stand block the audience's view?
- ▶ Could the performers see each other?
- ▶ Could their stage arrangement have been different?
- ▶ Would risers or rostra help?

MUSIC
- ▶ How was the overall shape of the music?
- ▶ How was the balance?
- ▶ How was the pacing?
- ▶ Are there any technical problems to be ironed out?

IMPACT OF THE PERFORMANCE
- ▶ How did the piece make you feel?
- ▶ What mental images or associations did you have?

'It was good to see if the enthusiasm you felt while performing was being put forward to the audience.'

DISCUSSION STRATEGIES

Feedback notes from each member of the audience can be handed directly to the performers immediately after the performance. If you are short of time this can be particularly useful.

The next session can start with responses to the written notes. Ask each person in turn for some feedback, beginning with the performers, who should be facing the audience. Make it clear that you expect a contribution from every one and ask them to prepare their thoughts for the discussion. Try to get them to go beyond their initial reactions and suspend their usual judgments and prejudices as they develop their critical thinking. Keep it specific.

Take care to establish an audience reaction loop that focuses on positives. It's tricky—we can't accept everything without some critical evaluation. On the other hand, don't discourage all spontaneous responses, especially where it is constructive criticism. Send messages such as 'it might have been stronger this way' and 'you might try this'.

'Strangely, I felt less nervous performing than I did talking about the performance afterwards with the group.'

'I felt that there was too much focus on the negative aspects of each other's performance and that the discussion became too opinionated. I think we need to respect each other's creativity and focus more on the positive elements of each other's performance.'

'The most important thing ... is being able to receive and respect the critical opinions of others.'

CHAPTER 5: CREATING PERFORMANCES FROM WORKSHOPS

MONITORING THE WORK

As the workshops progress, a lot of material is generated in the performances by the end of each session as the creative energy of the group is brought to life. This material needs to be constantly monitored, both by the leader and by the group. Ask the group members to make notes after each session about:

▶ What happened?
▶ What worked in your and your group's performance?
▶ What didn't work in your and your group's performance?
▶ What did you notice in other people's performances?
▶ What moments should be revisited or included in a public performance?
▶ Were there any connections you made to other aspects of your work?

As the leader you can also make notes—this will feed into your thinking on groups and their dynamics. I use small index cards, which can be stored in boxes. All the performance pieces and their personnel can be recorded on the cards. When the time comes to begin structuring the material for the show, these cards can be laid out in different orders and tested by the group. It may be that one or two of the pieces become a piece for the whole class. Perhaps some linking material needs to be generated to move from one piece to the next. The group may want every moment of their performance predetermined and rehearsed, or they may want to leave areas open to improvisation.

RECORDING AND PLAYBACK

As mentioned earlier, audio recording is a really useful tool but the equipment has to be of good quality. You can get excellent results with a minidisc recorder. Minidisc is the replacement technology for cassette and has a lot of advantages:

▶ Tracks can be cut up, pasted together and re-ordered;
▶ It's easy to directly transfer the tracks into computer sound-editing programs;
▶ The non-linear format means instant access to any point for playback, so there is no waiting in front of the class for the tape to rewind;
▶ The unit itself is tiny—smaller than a portable CD player.

If a minidisc isn't available you can still get good results using a cassette deck with microphone inputs. A stereo microphone will work well in a cassette deck's microphone inputs (the microphones sold for minidiscs are excellent).

Avoid using a tape recorder with an automatic recording level, which means that it adjusts the sound level as it records. A tape deck with a 'rec level' adjustment knob allows you to manually set the recording level in reference to the loudest sound the group is likely to make. If there is no 'rec level' knob, the recorder probably has an automatic recording level, so avoid using it!

Make a point of recording all performances. Include a verbal introduction: 'Friday, April 2; Neil, Helen, Kirstie and Andy; texture piece number one' etc. Listen to the pieces between sessions and schedule playback time into the course plan or session structure. As the weeks progress you can 'mock up' final performance materials in edited versions, to help with deciding on the content of the final show.

DECIDING ON CONTENT

At the end of each session 10 to 20 minutes of material might be generated and performed. If you run ten classes this could be over 200 minutes of material—assuming a 20-minute final show, you've got ten times more than you need. Something's got to go!

> 'Large group decision making is really hard if all members are to have a voice.'

In determining the content for final performances, I have tested many methods from authoritarian dictator (sorry, musical director) to a full democracy with committees, sub-committees and elected representatives. I have now settled on taking a directorial role and making a lot of editing and culling decisions. A balance can be struck by conducting whiteboard sessions where material is proposed, listed and voted on as a first step in reducing the 200 minutes to, say, forty or so. Refinement can follow. The group can prepare for this session in advance by referring to their own notes and remembering significant pieces and moments in the class that they could imagine making the leap from class to public performance. Establish a cut-off mark and lose any material that doesn't get over the line. See appendix two for examples of draft and final running orders which I have used.

LETTING GO

An important aspect of performance making is learning to let go. If students rehearse a piece over several trying days, they may still like to see the piece in the show, but perhaps the show's better off without it. The decision to include or exclude pieces has to serve the ideal of creating a wonderful group piece, and this is more important than personal likes and dislikes or the desire to keep everyone happy. It's not possible for everyone to be 100 per cent happy about the final shape of the show—but once the content has been determined, it's crucial that everyone commits to it and gives it their best. Let go of individual dissatisfaction and make it work as a team effort!

PUTTING ON A SHOW

Putting on a performance requires attention to a lot of details. Responsibilities can be divided and allocated to teams. Here are some things to consider:

VENUE

▶ Staging: How many chairs do you need? Have you checked the sight lines to ensure that the audience can see easily? Do you need rostra? Where will the audience sit or stand or move to?
▶ Lighting: Do you need to read music? Can everyone's faces be seen? Does the audience need to read a program?
▶ Audio: Is amplification needed? Do you want house music before and after the performance? Do you need any tape or CD cues?

▶ Access: How do we move equipment in? How does the audience get in?

PUBLICITY

▶ Mail out: What is a reasonable deadline? Who will write the text for promotional material and for the media release? Who will do the layout and design?

▶ Radio and print media: Can you get some free publicity via a story in a newspaper or a radio interview? Who wants to chase this up?

▶ Posters and fliers: Who will do the design and layout? Who will confirm information such as date, time, venue, venue address, performance title, description and booking details?

▶ Distribution: Who will put up some posters? Who will email out publicity? Who will post out invitations and fliers?

PRODUCTION

▶ Rehearsal schedule: This should include time for sound checking, lighting adjustments, setting up and rehearsing. Ideally you will have access to the venue a day or two before the performance.

▶ Stage management: It's a good idea to have a plan for stage management and for someone to look after it.

The performance is the ultimate focus of the workshop, and hopefully, it will be an enjoyable and challenging experience for all the participants. The delights of the rehearsal room will translate into something interesting to watch and listen to, usually to the surprise of the participants.

'Out of the corner of my eye I noticed smiles on people's faces.'

The String Can Quartet performing at the Victorian Arts Centre in 1996 (left to right: Graeme Leak, Jane Fisher, Tim Dargaville and Phil McLeod). (Photographer: Noel Butcher.)

PART TWO: WORKSHOP TECHNIQUES

The Percussion Maintenance Team at the Queensland Biennial
Festival of Music in 1999. (Photographer: Graeme Leak.)

CHAPTER 6: ISOLATION EXERCISES

The following three chapters contain a variety of isolation and stretching work that I have found useful. The pictures can be used as a quick reference and the instructions are simple. There is enough information for inexperienced readers to 'have a go' and gain some benefits, but I recommend professional instruction if you are seeking a deeper understanding of these exercises.

As with any physical activity, care must be taken not to ask participants to perform stretches that could bring about an injury. Your own level of knowledge and experience has to be taken into account if you want to lead a group in these kinds of activities. Physical safety is a big responsibility that ultimately rests with the individual. As group leader it's a good idea to discuss this before commencing any exercises, and those participants with injuries or afflictions should seek medical advice.

'First we warmed up. This was good because it got rid of any nerves and we regained focus.'

Stand in the neutral position firmly with feet parallel and hip width apart. Spread the toes, and imagine the feet as the roots of a tree, planted firmly in the soil.

Think of each foot as a triangle, its three points being the heel and each side of the ball of the foot. Rock gently back and forth, side to side and around in a circle. Feel the weight shift between the six points of the two triangles. Settle on a position where each of the six points has an equal feeling of pressure.

Activate the knees by pulling the kneecaps up with the thigh muscles. Try to maintain this action while still being aware of the weight being evenly distributed on the triangles of both feet.

Think of the pelvis as a shallow dish containing water, located at the top of the legs. Tip the dish forwards and backwards, side to side and in circles. Settle on a position where the water is level. Make sure that your weight is evenly distributed on all six points of the feet, that your knees are activated and your pelvis is level.

Imagine the spine as a tree trunk. It's as thick as the wrist and runs up through the neck to support the head. The skull rests on the spine with a ball joint.

Drop the head forward and backward, side to side, exploring the 360-degree movement that is possible with this amazing connection of head to spine. We usually only use a tiny proportion of the movements that this joint is capable of, mainly the 'yes' and 'no' gestures.

Imagine circular movements in every possible direction. Settle on a position where the forehead is slightly in front of the chin.

Activate the arms by stretching the fingers. Spread them and bring them together to make a flat board at the end of the arm. Open the chest by rolling the shoulders back slightly. Shift the attention back to the weight on the feet.

Transfer all weight to the left foot, and raise the right foot by bending the right knee. At the same time drop the hips slightly by bending the left knee. You are now standing on your left foot, with your left knee bent and your right foot about 10 centimetres from the floor.

Wiggle the toes of the right foot. How much independent movement do you have with the toes? Feel the joints of each toe by moving them. What kinds of movement are possible with toes? Can they move in more than one plane? Can they make circular movements?

Shift focus to the right ankle. Move the joint up and down, side to side, in circles to the left, to the right and in every possible direction. Explore the possibilities of this joint.

Shift focus to the right knee—a hinge joint. Find its limits of movement—note that it can't bend forward and only moves in the one plane.

Shift focus to the right hip—another ball joint. Move it up and down, back and forth, side to side, in circles to the left, in circles to the right and in every way you can. Try small and big movements, fast and slow. Transfer your weight to the right foot, and give the left leg a big shake, and rest on both feet.

Repeat with the weight on the right foot and left foot off the ground. Explore the left toes, ankles, knees, hips and return to even weight on both feet after giving the right leg a shake.

Shift focus to the fingers. Move the joints one by one in each finger. How independent are they? How do they compare to the toes? There are enormous expressive capabilities in the fingers. Explore them. Think about the opposing thumb and where you would be without it. Massage each joint. Feel the spaces within each joint. Think about the way the bones knit together.

Shift focus to the wrists—another set of ball joints. Move them up and down, back and forth, side to side, in circles to the left, in circles to the right and in every way that you can.

Shift focus to the elbows. They are similar to the knees—simple hinges with limits. What are the constraints of elbow movement?

Shift focus to the shoulders. They are similar to the hips. Move them up and down, back and forth, side to side, in circles to the left, in circles to the right and in every way you can.

Shift focus to the stomach and abdomen. What movement is possible there?

Shift your attention to the chest. Expand and contract, push out and in, up and down.

Shift focus to the face. Move the jaw up and down, side to side. Notice how it connects to the skull. Wiggle the ears, nose and forehead.

Turn to the next person and give them a light 'reminder' massage, starting at the toes and moving through all the body parts in the same order: toes, ankles, knees, hips, pelvis, fingers, wrists, elbows, shoulders, stomach, chest, neck, face and head.

The purpose of the massage is to have an external reference to aid your internal visualisation of your body structure. When you reach the stomach and chest, place one hand at the front of the body and one on the back to demonstrate to your partner how wide their body is.

Finish by lightly pulling the hair at the very top of their head as though you are lengthening their spine.

CHAPTER 7: FLOOR STRETCHES

(1) SPINAL TWIST

Place right ankle in front of left.

Move right shoulder forward, left shoulder back. Inhale—extend spine up, lift head higher. Exhale—increase turn-stretch.

Repeat with left ankle in front of right.

Move left shoulder forward, right shoulder back. Inhale—extend spine up, lift head higher. Exhale—increase turn-stretch.

(2) FORWARD BEND I

Place right
ankle in front of
left, inhale—
stretch up.

Exhale—bend
forward,
bringing
abdomen
towards thighs.

Breathe and
hold. Repeat
with left ankle
in front.

(3) FORWARD BEND 2

Press feet
together,
extend spine
upwards and
inhale.

Exhale—bend
forward.

Hold a few
breaths and
return to the
upright
position slowly.

(4) FORWARD BEND 3

Place right arm and right ankle in front. Inhale —extend up.

Exhale—bend forward.

Repeat, with left arm and left ankle in front.

(5) FORWARD BEND 4

Inhale—stretch up.

Exhale—bend forward, keeping lower back straight.

(6) CALF AND HAMSTRING STRETCH

Tuck right
ankle into left
thigh and
extend left leg
forward.

Bend forward
slowly, only as
far as
comfortable.
Keep lower
back straight.

Repeat, with
left ankle
tucked into
right thigh and
right leg
forward.

(7) UPPER CHEST AND ARM STRETCH

Extend left arm up and move right hand to centre of back.

Make left hand meet right hand. If your hands don't meet, use a strap or a cloth.

Repeat, extending right arm up and moving left hand to centre of back.

(8) PELVIS LIFT

Relax on the floor.

With hands by your side and palms down, exhale— prepare to lift.

Inhale—raise pelvis up. Arch back and hold. Exhale—lower slowly.

(9) SIDE BEND

Inhale—stretch
upwards
through your
arms.

Exhale—bend
to right side.

Inhale—stretch
upwards
through your
arms.

Exhale—bend
to left side.

(10) GENTLE BACK TWIST

Lie on back
with arms out.
Draw knees up,
shift buttocks
off-centre to
the right.

Lower knees to
the left, turn
head to the
right and keep
shoulders in
contact with
floor.

Repeat in
reverse with
buttocks off-
centre to the
left.

(11) LEG STRETCH 1

Graeme Leak
PERFORMANCE MAKING

Draw knees up.

Place left ankle on right knee.

Using hands looped around lower right thigh, bring right knee forward.

Repeat with right ankle on left knee.

(12) LEG STRETCH 2

Use a strap around left foot to move left knee towards chest, keeping right leg extended.

With strap still around left foot, straighten leg and gently pull towards face, keeping leg straight.

Repeat with right leg.

CHAPTER 8: STANDING STRETCHES

(1) DOWN-FACE DOG POSE

Lie face down with feet hip-width apart and some weight on toes.
Place hands face down beneath shoulders.

Straighten arms and bend legs so that knees rest on floor. Keep back straight and parallel to floor.

Straighten legs, with weight on balls of feet. Gradually lower heels onto floor.

(2) SPINAL ROLL

Stand in the neutral position.

Lift head and drop it gently forward in stages, as if you are releasing one spinal disk at a time.

Continue to release spinal disks one at a time, very slowly.

Relax and hang.

Return to upright position very slowly, as if you are rebuilding the spine.

(3) BACKWARD AND FORWARD BEND

Stand in the neutral position. Place hands behind thighs.

Slowly bend backward.

Support your back with your arms. Look up. Breathe deeply.

Return to the neutral position then slowly bend forward.

(4) FORWARD BEND

Stand with the feet wide apart and move arms forward, up to shoulder level. Inhale.

Move arms out to the side. Exhale.

Bend at the waist and move torso down, swinging arms back. Inhale.

When arms are straight up, exhale. Return to the upright position.

(5) PELVIS AND HIP ROTATION

Stand with
hands on hips.

Move your hips
forward then
round to the
right, while
moving your
torso down to
your left.

Move your hips
back while
bending your
torso forward.

Move your hips
forward then
round to the
left while
moving your
torso back to an
upright
position.

(6) MERIDIAN STRETCH

Stand in the neutral position.

Inhale as you move your left arm up to the side, with your right hand holding your right foot and bringing it towards the buttocks.

Hold. Then exhale as you move your left arm down and release your right foot, returning to neutral position.

Repeat, raising your right arm and with your left hand holding your left foot.

(7) CIRCULAR STRETCH

Stand with feet wide apart. Inhale.

Bend to the left, raising your right arm and placing your left hand on left thigh. Exhale.

Bend at the waist and move torso towards front with your arms down.

Inhale.

Move torso towards your right until your left arm is raised. Exhale.

Return to upright position.

(8) TRIKONÁSANA

Stand in the neutral position.

Jump wide, placing feet wide apart and parallel.

Turn left foot out and right foot in, and look left.

Exhale—bend to the left, bringing left hand to left shin or ankle, and look up.

Inhale—come up.

Turn to the centre.

- ▶ Workshop a few descriptions on a whiteboard or a large sheet of paper, trying to achieve objective language focusing on the musical qualities of the sounds;
- ▶ Get people to construct their own list of the sounds heard during the walk outside following this model.

> 'With my eyes closed my sense of hearing seems magnified. A panorama of sound is now available, which was there all the while but I simply didn't notice it.'

GUESS THE SOUND

Make sounds for the group. They can listen with eyes closed or sounds can be produced from behind a screen. Ask them to write down how they think the sound was being made. Try using general descriptions such as 'wood on glass' and 'metal on metal'.

Some suggestions:
- ▶ dropping pebbles in water;
- ▶ rubbing a balloon;
- ▶ sharpening a pencil;
- ▶ walking on dry leaves;
- ▶ pouring rice into a metal bowl;
- ▶ crumpling paper;
- ▶ ripping paper;
- ▶ clicking a pen cap on and off;
- ▶ fastening and unfastening a zipper;
- ▶ using a stapler;
- ▶ jiggling keys;
- ▶ tearing aluminium foil;
- ▶ unwrapping a lolly;
- ▶ tapping a pencil on a coffee cup;
- ▶ slapping books together;
- ▶ dropping a shoe;
- ▶ dragging a ruler against a wall.

You can rotate the role of making sounds from person to person.

> 'As long as we are listening to each other the piece should work really well.'

(2) MOVING
STAND THERE AND DO NOTHING
Divide the group into two: audience and performers. Announce the first performance task: 'Stand in front of the watchers and do nothing for 60 seconds'. Call out a second task: 'Stand and count the bricks on the wall behind the audience'. Swap. When both groups have finished, discuss:

As a performer:
▶ Were you worried about what others thought of you?
▶ What strategies did you use to deal with the task?

As a watcher:
▶ Were the performances boring?
▶ Was the first task less interesting to watch than the second?

When participants have a clear task to perform, they seem less worried about how others perceive them, and when they are less worried, they are better performers. Usually some in the group will find a point of focus and hold it, while others may look fidgety and self-conscious. Stress the fact that being onstage means that you are under a microscope—nothing goes unnoticed, and even tiny eye movements can have an impact on the audience.

AIMLESS WALKING
Both the aimless and directed walking exercises involve the group moving in the space while listening for

instructions from the leader. This exercise builds peripheral awareness and creates a sense of working as an ensemble. It can also mark the important transition from 'ordinary' time to 'performance-making' time.

► Start the exercise by assuming the neutral position.
► The workshop leader should outline the format of the instructions that will follow.
► The leader should ask participants to rock gently forward and backward until falling forward into a slow walk.
► Participants should walk aimlessly around the room, and then follow the walk instructions (see below) announced by the workshop leader:
  ► Say, 'After I say "go", you will ignore/ acknowledge/move from slow to fast/start and stop' and then say, 'go';
  ► After some time, say, 'freeze';
  ► Call a new walk instruction and say 'go'.
► Some instructions can be called while the group is moving.

IGNORE
Ignore others that you encounter.

ACKNOWLEDGE
Politely acknowledge others that you pass, as though you are strangers in the city streets.

SLOW/MEDIUM/FAST
Bring the pace of the walk up, and give it some purpose, as if you are walking briskly to your bus. Walk more quickly, as if you're running late and your energy is lifting.

You're really running now—you can't miss that bus. Return to a slow pace.

START/STOP

Variation 1: Insert pauses of varying lengths of time. When pausing, remain still and focused. Restart on impulse.

Variation 2: If anyone stops, everyone must stop. If, when everyone is stopped, someone starts, all must start. Anyone is free to start and stop (and so control the room) at any time.

Variation 3: As you see someone, stop and stare at them for a moment, then break away and move on. Try not to laugh. Become aware in your peripheral vision of all members of the group. Work towards the whole room stopping (in pairs, staring at each other briefly), and the whole room starting to move again. Try to vary the time spent stopping and starting.

COMBINATIONS

Devise combinations of ignore/acknowledge, slow/medium/fast, start/stop and pauses. Either prescribe these or ask the group to devise their own.

DIRECTED WALKING

Following the same format as for the aimless walking exercise, experiment with these instructions which are to be announced by the workshop leader.

POINT OF FOCUS

Instead of wandering aimlessly, find a point of focus on a wall or distant point. This is your goal. Set your sights on it and walk to it with purpose and conviction. When you arrive at your goal, turn, find another point of focus, and walk to it in the same way.

PARALLEL

Walk only in straight lines parallel to the walls. Change direction by turning at 90- and 180-degree angles.

CURVED
Walk in curves only, with no straight lines. Vary between tight, medium and broad curves, and between curving to the left and to the right.

JAGGED
Walk briskly in straight lines with turns in any direction, creating a jagged pattern. Vary the pace and include pauses.

COMBINATIONS
Mix and match parallel, curvy, jagged and random walking with fast, medium and slow paces. Sometimes acknowledge others and sometimes ignore them. Try the start/stop variations and insert pauses. Prescribe combinations or have the participants change at random and on impulse. Maintain peripheral awareness at all times.

LEADING WITH BODY PARTS
Lead with body parts. Imagine that you are a vehicle slicing through water and present one body part as the leading edge of your vehicle. Try leading with your:
► nose;
► ankles;
► hips;
► shoulders;
► knees;
► elbows;
► forehead;
► chin.

HIGH STATUS/LOW STATUS
Walk around with the chest out. Walk with chest in (curved shoulders, droopy head), then discuss the feelings evoked by the two styles of movement:

► What kind of relationship to the space is created? Why?

► Which looks and feels better on stage?

► Did participants with 'chests out' tend to gravitate towards the centre of the room? Did those with 'chests in' tend to move towards the edges of the room? Why?

(3) MAKING SOUNDS
SEND THE SOUND AROUND (IN A CIRCLE)

Stand in a circle. The leader starts the game by holding an imaginary sound in his or her hands, making eye contact with someone opposite, and then 'throwing' it towards that person.

For example, try struggling to hold a huge boulder in your hands and then heaving it with grunts and groans to the next player, who catches it in the same way. Once caught, the boulder might become a feather that is tossed lightly in the air, and all eyes would then watch it flutter across the circle. The catcher would mimic the same light, puffy sound as was used to throw it.

It is a good idea to ban farts and burps from the outset.

SEND THE CLAP AROUND

Stand in a circle. Ask everyone to focus on the person immediately to his or her right. The leader 'sends' a clap around the circle to the left, using a very clear, rotating body movement to indicate direction. As a player sees the person to their right sending the clap, they quickly pass it on.

Keep the focus to your right and concentrate on the sound of the clap moving around. Try to get it going as quickly as possible. With practice, it can get really fast.

Variations include:

▶ Direction change: Anyone can change the direction of the clap at any time. If you don't want to pass it to your left, you can send it back. Use the body to clearly indicate direction. Continue until it gets faster.

▶ 'Shh': Use the sound 'shh' instead of a clap. Try to connect with each other so we hear one long 'ssshhhhhh' sound travelling around the circle.

▶ 'Shh' to the right, clap to the left: Send 'shh' to the right, allow it to get established for a while then introduce a clap to the left. It is difficult, especially for the person who gets both at once, but it is possible with practice. Focus.

MUSICAL ROUNDS

Musical rounds are excellent vocal warm-ups. One of my favourite two-part rounds is 'Mr Bach':

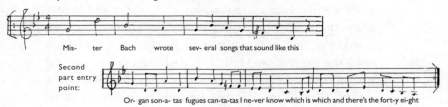

Mis- ter Bach wrote sev- eral songs that sound like this

Second part entry point:

Or- gan son-a- tas fugues can-ta-tas I ne-ver know which is which and there's the fort-y ei-ght

'THREE BLIND MICE' WITH VARIATIONS

Sing 'Three Blind Mice' in unison a few times with gusto. Then offer the following suggestions starting with the call, 'now we will sing as though...':

▶ 'They are chasing you';
▶ 'You are an army sergeant';
▶ 'You hate them';
▶ 'You are putting them to sleep (as in a lullaby)';
▶ 'You and the mice are drunk!'.

Discuss the effects of the variations on the dynamics, duration, attack, tempo, accuracy etc. (See the glossary.)

CHAPTER 10: GAMES

(1) NAME GAMES
Use these games with a new group, to get to know each others' names.

BALL NAME GAME
Stand in a circle. Using a tennis ball, make eye contact with a person opposite you, say their name and throw them the ball. If you can't remember their name, say 'sorry' and they will remind you. Be clear and confident with the calling and throwing. As the game settles and a rhythm develops, introduce a second tennis ball, then a third. Try to keep focused as you wait for a ball to come your way.

Now repeat the game, this time while walking randomly around the room. Call the name and wait until the person is looking at you before you throw. Begin with one ball, then two and three. Overlay some instructions from the directed walking exercise to add variation.

Now try walking in pairs and sticking together, still throwing three tennis balls and names around. Then try walking in groups of three and if there are enough people in the group, try walking in groups of four.

BARRIER NAME GAME

Split the group into two even teams, sitting on the floor facing each other. The leader plus one helper can hold a blanket or sheet as a barrier between the two groups. Each group silently positions a player up close to the barrier, the barrier is suddenly dropped and they are face to face. The first one to call the name of the other wins a point for their side.

SAY YOUR NAME

Each participant simply announces his or her name, going around the circle. During this simple yet surprisingly difficult performance task, aim for:

▶ 100 per cent commitment;
▶ no laughter;
▶ no embarrassment.

Repeat until each performer is clear and focused.

VARIATION 1

Add a movement gesture to the performance.

VARIATION 2

Add a movement and a sound to the performance.

(2) PLAYGROUND GAMES

TIPPITY (TAG, TIGGER AND FREEZE TAG)

One person is 'it'. When that person tips or tags another, that person is frozen. The not-yet-frozen players can release frozen players by:

▶ tagging them;
▶ crawling between the legs of the frozen ones;
▶ appointing a small group of unfreezers, who keep their identity secret from 'it'.

BRITISH BULLDOG

Divide the space into three areas: a zone for captured players with a safe zone on either side.

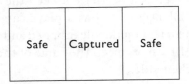

'It' stands in the central zone. Players attempt to cross from one safe area to the other without being captured by 'it'. Once tagged, they also try to capture others. The winner is the last free player.

BALL GAME (50 UP)

Position the players evenly throughout the workspace. Punch a volleyball into the air, and work together as a team to keep it aloft. Everyone counts in unison at each whack, trying to get as far as possible before the ball hits the floor. Ten is bad, fifteen is getting better, twenty is good, thirty is excellent and fifty is unbelievable! Call the numbers really loudly.

(3) STATUS GAMES

Status games illustrate the potency of various attitudes on stage. While seemingly unconnected to music, the images of this game can remain in the memory and influence stage presence.

'A's AND 'B's

▶ Divide the group into half audience and half performers.

▶ Name half the performers 'A' and the other half, 'B'.

▶ 'A's have high status. They ignore the desperate attempts by 'B's for eye contact. Perform for a minute or so and then swap (so that 'B's ignore 'A's).

▶ Swap audience and performers, and repeat.

▶ Discuss the observations by audience and performers.

MASTER/SERVANT

The master sits in a chair. All others in the room must remain lower than the master. Never let the master see your back. The master can command any servant to do anything and must continue to order and bully servants relentlessly. Servants must comply with every demand and act out the instruction. If the master is not happy with a servant's performance he or she can order the servant to die, at which point the servant must die, spectacularly.

If a servant makes the master laugh, then that servant becomes the new master; the old master becomes just another servant and all dead servants can come alive.

(4) DRAMA GAMES

TELLING STORIES 'A WORD AT A TIME'

In a circle, the group tells a single story, with each person saying one word at a time. Keep the pace up—if you hesitate you have to retire. Say the first word that comes into your head. Let go of what you hoped it might be. For example, you may say 'once' (thinking 'once upon a time'), and the next person may say 'there' (thinking 'once there was a little girl') and the next person may say 'stood' (thinking 'once there stood a row of trees'). Don't stop to think about it—just say the word and let the story unfold.

Don't try to be clever, or funny, or pre-determine what you are going to say. Listen—respond just to the words before you, and add your word so that it makes sense with all the other words.

STATUES

Teams of two participants work together as sculptor and mannequin, with the sculptor being able to move the mannequin to any position and admire the outcome. The mannequin must be entirely cooperative and very still. Work in silence—communication is by touch only, with no verbal instructions.

When the sculptor feels that the sculpture is finished, he or she steps back and stands at the edge of the room to admire the work. When all sculptors are finished we have a room full of statues. Swap and repeat.

VARIATION I

Only communicate by 'force field'. That is, never actually touch the mannequin. Instead, put your hand very close to the area you want to move and by magic, it will move exactly as you want it to.

VARIATION 2

When all the sculptures are complete, the sculptors stand back and admire their work. After some time and on cue from the leader, the mannequins are asked to move in a way suggested to them by their pose. The room will come alive with strange creatures.

MAKE A PICTURE

The leader identifies a scene for the group to imagine, for example, 'a supermarket' or 'the beach' or 'the photocopying room'. All stand in the audience area of the space looking at the stage. One person at a time walks in, announcing what they are in the picture. For example, if we are looking at a toyshop, I would stroll in and stretch out my arms and say, 'I am a kite hanging from the ceiling'. Then the next person may move to an opposite corner to me and say, 'I am the cash register' and so on. The picture is still (not moving). It's finished when all performers are in the picture.

OBJECTS

Split the group into subsets of three or four. Each group has to work together to quickly make an object.

For example, if the leader says 'computer', one person would jump on all fours and say that his or her back is the keyboard. Two others would work together to make a screen out of their arms, positioned behind and above the keyboard. A person with hair in a long plait could be the mouse and use his or her plait as the cable to connect to the keyboard.

Read from a list of objects and have everyone work quickly. At the conclusion of each image give all the groups a chance to look at what the other groups have created. Any object will do, for example, a windsurfer, a blender, a bicycle, a piano, a Christmas tree, a pincushion or an aquarium.

MACHINE

Get the whole group to work together to make a machine. It can be anything at all—something fantastic is good, like a machine that manufactures snow clouds, or a machine to clean the filthy pots of the giant at the top of the beanstalk (they are as big as the room and caked with burnt food). Start by standing on the edge of the empty stage. The first person enters the stage and offers a sound and movement loop. Everyone considers it for a while and then the next person joins, adding the next bit to the machine. Take your time—only one person should enter at a time, consider each new addition and ponder where they fit in.

When the machine is complete, it can speed up to a frenzy and then break down spectacularly.

VARIATION 1

Divide the group into half actors and half musicians with instruments and/or voices, and play again.

VARIATION 2

Transfer to all instruments and/or all voices and play again.

NAME-WRITING DANCE

Ask each person to write their name in the air, using a different part of the body to make each letter. Try to write each letter in a different three-dimensional plane and in a different scale.

The leader can demonstrate the game.

For example, I can write a 'g' with my elbow on an imaginary blackboard in front of me, then I can trace an 'r' with my toe in the sand, then I can use my knee to scratch an 'a' on the sloping ramp to my left, then I can use the top of my head to wipe an 'e' on the ceiling.

Split the group in half, with half watching and half performing the piece. Swap. Discuss.

VARIATION I

Perform to a CD (any CD, any style of music) and repeat the split class performance. Change the CD to a contrasting style and swap. Discuss again. Note down the conclusions of the group, and keep an eye on those who have trouble staying focused on the task.

VARIATION 2

As with the machine, divide into half musicians and half dancers, and repeat.

VARIATION 3

Perform the name-writing dance with instruments and/ or voice. Think laterally and visually.

CHAPTER 11: MUSIC SKILLS

Musical performance deals primarily with two parameters, rhythm and pitch, in real time. The following skills in rhythm and pitch are universal to any style of music and to any level of performer. They are based on the idea of implanting reference points in the mind and body that can be accurately recalled. If one pitch is ingrained and known, all other pitches can be found relative to the known pitch. Similarly, if one tempo (speed) is known, all other tempos can be found relative to the known tempo.

(1) PULSE = 60 BEATS PER MINUTE

Ask the group: what does the word pulse mean? Wait for a variety of responses and associated words. Decide on a definition that suits everybody. Could it be the fundamental, internal and underlying beat? Could it be the engine room? Or is it the life force?

Western music is influenced by our approach to organising time. We divide the days into hours and subdivide the hours into minutes and seconds. Similarly in music, we divide the bars into beats and the beats into rhythms.

The musical clock, the metronome, is a great tool to assist in developing a strong sense of tempo, or beats per minute (b.p.m.). Watches and clocks can also be used.

EXERCISE 1

Set a metronome going and make guesses at the tempo. Put up your hands up to nominate the b.p.m., take votes after all the nominations are put forward. A person with a highly developed perception of time can accurately guess any tempo. Getting close is good enough at this point. Applaud the winners.

EXERCISE 2

Ask the group to watch the second hand of a clock (or their watches) and absorb the feeling of 60 b.p.m. Do this for a while in silence, and then play this pulse together with the feet in a circle. Turn a metronome on and try to keep the whole group focused on it (a metronome with a swinging arm is needed for this, as a flashing light metronome gives no 'in-between' indication of the tempo). Listen and adjust.

EXERCISE 3

Repeat exercise one with a few different speeds. Start with directly related ones, like 120 b.p.m. and 30 b.p.m., then 90 b.p.m. and 180 b.p.m., then mix it right up. You can use watches as a 60 b.p.m. reference while doing this.

Set the following tasks:
▶ Each day use every spare minute to first imagine 60 b.p.m., tap it out loud, check your tempo against either a metronome or a clock (with a ticking second hand) and then adjust your timing. You can do this anywhere, anytime, for example, while you are on public transport or in a cafe.

▶ Watch a digital clock (with no second indication on it) and begin counting seconds when a new number turns over. See if you can reach 61 as the next number turns over.

▶ While watching either a metronome or a clock as a 60 b.p.m. reference, clap 30 b.p.m. and 120 b.p.m. to get used to the nearest relatives of 60 b.p.m.

After just a few days it is possible to get a strong sense of knowing 60 b.p.m., which can then be accurately recalled without reference to a clock or metronome for the rest of your life. Once you are familiar with 60 b.p.m., you can relate all other speeds to it. You can become a human metronome!

(2) A = 440 CYCLES PER SECOND

The A above middle C has a frequency of 440 cycles per second (c.p.s.). This is the note that an orchestra tunes up to and musicians usually sound it before an ensemble performance. Once we know this note, all other notes can be found.

Alard Maling, my timpani teacher and one of Australia's greatest timpanists, told me to hang an A chime bar at the end of my bed and to kick it when I woke up so it was the first sound I heard for the day. I didn't do it but he swore that it worked for him. Maybe you could try it!

EXERCISE

Imagine the sound of A above middle C. Perhaps think of the oboe sound. Listen to it in your mind and focus on it. When you can hear it clearly with your inner hearing, sing it out loud.

Now check it against a tuning fork or a keyboard instrument. If you don't know where this is on a keyboard, ask someone to show you. Were you higher, lower, spot on, or perhaps a tiny bit above or below? Adjust, and sing the note again until you can hear that you are perfectly in tune.

Do this several times a day (every time you walk past a piano, for example, or on the bus or in the shower with your tuning fork). Very soon the note A will be permanently ingrained and easy to recall. (Be sure that the keyboard you use is in tune. Old pianos can be very flat, so check with a tuning fork.)

(3) TONES AND SEMITONES

Tones and semitones are the basic building blocks of pitch. In combination with the ability to sing A from memory, any note can be found by working out how many steps away from A it is, provided you can accurately sing whole and half steps, or tones and semitones. You'll need a reference instrument for the following exercise.

EXERCISE

The leader invents signs to indicate whole step up, half step up, whole step down and half step down, for example:

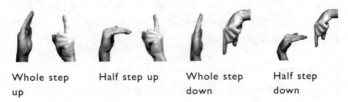

Whole step up   Half step up   Whole step down   Half step down

The group begins by singing A and the conductor directs (using the agreed sign) the note one whole step up, then returns to A. Next the conductor directs one whole step down and returns to A. Repeat for half steps.

Tones up and down

Semitones up and down

So far, we have sung two notes above A and two notes below. Including A this is five notes. Now the conductor combines these five available notes to improvise melodies around A. Guest conductors may also lead the group.

Here is an example of one possible improvisation using a five-note melody.

Discuss whether there is a certain freedom implied within the severe limitation of only five notes. What about the duration of the notes? Should we try some short notes, or a rhythm?

Try working on this individually as often as possible between sessions. Once again, the sequence is:

▶ imagine A and sing it;
▶ check it against a reference and adjust;
▶ imagine whole steps above and below and then sing them;
▶ use a keyboard to check, adjust for accuracy and repeat;
▶ do the same for half steps;
▶ mix and match whole and half steps above and below A (using five notes including A). Invent melodies and add rhythm and dynamics, then sing the song.

(4) MAJOR, MINOR, DIMINISHED AND AUGMENTED TRIADS

Once you have completed the foundation work on A = 440 c.p.s. and tones and semitones, then you are ready to experiment with the effects of different combinations of notes. Here, we will be exploring the triad, which is a set of three notes comprising the root (or tonic) and the third and fifth notes of the scale. (See the glossary.)

EXERCISE

Divide the group into sopranos, tenors and altos, and basses. Then create a close-position major triad on A. This means that the tenors and altos will be on middle C♯, the basses on the A below that, and the sopranos on the E above that.

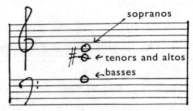

Listen to the chord and get it really in tune. Check against a keyboard regularly. Purposefully wander away from the centre of your note and hear the beats with imperfect pitch. Allow your ears to listen and tune the triad to perfection. Stay with this for quite a while (it's quite enjoyable to realise how easy it is to sing in tune if you just listen). Now the leader directs semitone or half-step movements of each note as follows.

▶ First, the fifth is moved up a semitone to make an augmented triad. Stay with the new triad for a while, getting used to its different sound and feel.

▶ Then, the fifth is moved back down to perfect, returning to the major triad.

▶ The third is moved down a step to create a minor triad. Stay with it for a while and listen and adjust to the difference.

▶ From the minor triad, the fifth can now move down to create the diminished triad. Stay there, listen and stay in tune. Notice how there is a feeling of tension. Why is it harder to keep this triad in tune?

▶ Now the bass note is moved down a semitone and we modulate to a new key, so that we are singing a new major triad on G♯.

The sequence is repeated. The sequence can also modulate in the other direction, with the bass note moving up a semitone when the triad is augmented to modulate to a new minor triad. The following illustrates the sequence in the key of G:

In close position:

major   augmented   major   minor   diminished   major

Open SATB voicing:

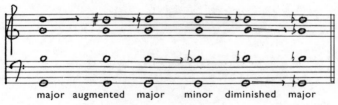

major   augmented   major   minor   diminished   major

The above can be played as a game, where the leader doesn't direct the semitone movements but each note-group decides when it will move to create the new triad. The rules are:

For the people singing the fifth:
▶ move up to the augmented triad only when a major third is sounding;

▶ move down to the diminished triad only when a minor third is sounding.

For the people singing the third:
▶ only move up to the major triad or down to the minor triad when a perfect fifth is sounding.

For the people singing the tonic:
▶ only move up when an augmented triad is sounding, or down when a diminished triad is sounding.

As an ongoing warm-up exercise and when the group becomes familiar with the tonalities, various voicings can be explored. Four part arrangements can be created, trying different notes in the bass with one note doubled. Which is the best note to double? How do really wide voicings sound? How is it different when the tonic isn't the bass note? Can this work be transferred to instruments?

CHAPTER 12: NOISE EXERCISES

NOISE

It is said that the difference between noise and music is whether we like it or not. If we don't like it, it's noise, and we don't want it in our aural environment.

Noise prevents the possibility of a clean backdrop for sounds. Sounds exist with clarity in environments where there is little or no background noise, which is why we have soundproof concert halls and recording studios.

DISCUSSION TOPICS

▶ What is noise?
▶ What is the difference between noise and music?
▶ Can noise be music?
▶ Is noise perhaps an individual judgment linked to perception and prejudice? For example, some people hear music in the sound of passing cars. Others only hear music in the sounds of recognisable instruments. Is noise anything that we don't want in music?
▶ Is it possible to sometimes learn to like a noise you thought you didn't like at first?

EXERCISE: NOISY INTERRUPTIONS

Select any piece of text. It's good to use something completely out of context, like a technical manual or a fishing handbook or a newspaper gossip column. Ask someone to read the text aloud.

Ask the group to generate noise (preferably continuous rather than percussive, for example, roars, whistles, loud singing, gibberish, conversation, engine sounds). Make the noise loud enough to mask the sound of the reader.

Start and stop this noise on a cue. Listen. Experiment with other kinds of noises, for example, murmurs, shuffling, coughing, and even one person whispering to another. At all times the group observes the effect of the noise.

What happens? What happens to the understanding of the text? What happens if a solo flute is playing as an aeroplane flies overhead? Discuss the notion of foreground sound, background sound and masking.

Repeat, and ask the reader to find ways to cut through the noise. What strategy proves useful? Compare the impact of higher sounds, louder sounds, higher and louder sounds, and lower and louder sounds.

Ask for a graphic representation of this piece to be drawn on a whiteboard. Anyone can contribute to the drawing until the group is happy with the illustration.

PERFORMANCE TASK

In smaller groups incorporate new elements into the exercise. Replace the text with, for example, a solo instrument, a conversation, a CD or a vocal duo. Mask this sound with, for example, the sound of instruments, audio equipment, domestic machinery or a motorbike. Organise these materials into a short performance, and draw a diagram of the piece to explain to others how to perform it.

CHAPTER 13: SILENCE EXERCISES

SILENCE

In 1952 John Cage wrote '4' 33" '. The performer sits at a piano and does nothing for 4 minutes and 33 seconds. Audiences for the piece tend to become very uncomfortable and feel obliged to fill the stillness by making sounds.

Performers are often afraid of silence. Like the Cage audience, they want to make sounds if there is too much stillness about. Many improvising musicians have a bad habit of playing too much, of 'plugging all the holes' and leaving no space for the sounds to live and breath. However, space/stillness/rest can be a powerful composing and performing tool, as the following exercises are designed to show.

DISCUSSION TOPICS

▶ Even in a totally soundproof room, the listener is alive, breathing, pumping blood. Is there such a thing as pure silence?
▶ Is there a difference between silence, stillness and rest?

EXERCISES

▶ Perform a one-minute version of '4' 33" '. Discuss the effect on both performer and audience.

▶ In a still room, drop a pin. Ask the group to close their eyes. Try different surfaces and differently-sized pins. Can each pin be heard? Is it different with your eyes closed?

▶ Ask the group to sit in one long line, all facing the front. One member goes to the front and attempts to make a sound so quiet that no one can hear it. Listeners close their eyes and raise their hand when they hear anything. Try using different instruments, voices or objects (a piece of paper, a shoe or whatever). Try to ensure at least some of the hands do not go up when a sound is made. This exercise highlights the incredible range of dynamics available for use in performance. Often the soft end of the dynamic spectrum is ignored. It is almost impossible to make a sound on stage that no one will hear. Greater use of this end of the spectrum serves to widen the available dynamic range, as louder sounds will be perceived with more impact if they exist in relation to truly quiet ones.

▶ Interpret this noise/silence continuum, where 42 units of time are alternately still and sounding in the following ratio:

PERFORMANCE TASKS

In smaller groups, refer to any or all of the exercises to make a piece that overcomes any residual anxiety about remaining still on stage. Totally silent pieces are encouraged, as is use of the softest possible utterances. The 42-unit ratio, or any other pre-determined sound/silence ratio, can be used. Simultaneous performances involving a few of the smaller groups may be possible.

CHAPTER 14:
PULSE EXERCISES

PULSE
The pulse of a piece of music is the underlying beat which drives it.

DISCUSSION TOPICS
▶ What does the word 'pulse' mean to you? List the responses on a board.
▶ What is pulse in relation to music?

INDEPENDENT PULSE
Listen to the rate of your breathing. Don't adjust anything, just relax and breathe normally. Imagine your inhale/exhale cycle as a loop. Now locate one point on this loop and click your fingers each time you reach that same point. With eyes closed continue to listen to your own breath as you click your fingers at the pre-determined point. Now shift your listening focus to include the combined sounds of everyone in the room doing the same thing.

VARIATIONS
(1) Replace the finger click with a different body-percussion sound of your own.

(2) Try a vocal sound instead of a percussion sound. Experiment with different durations and dynamics.

(3) Only play a sound on every second, or third, or fourth breath. Mix vocal and percussion sounds.

(4) Devise your own scheme of when to play and when not to, for example: 'In a six breath cycle I'll make a sound on breath one and breath five only'. Try different ratios of silence to sound. Discuss the differences.

DISCUSSION TOPICS

After trying the variations, discuss:

▶ What kind of pulse is it?

▶ Where do you usually hear this kind of pulse?

Independent pulse occurs around us all the time, in both the natural and built environments. You hear it on a factory floor, in city streets, on building sites or in the calm and tranquility of the bush. The machines, the people and the bush animals all sound in relation to their own unique, independent pulse.

PERFORMANCE TASK

Working as a large group, transfer the vocal/body pieces to instruments. Keep it simple and limit the gestures. Keep the performances short (1–2 minutes), propose variations and try them out, record the pieces and listen to them either straight afterwards or at a later session.

UNIFIED PULSE

Most musical performances have an agreed, or unified, pulse rate that the performers lock into.

EXERCISE

Place a metronome on the floor in the middle of the circle sounding a 60 b.p.m. pulse. Establish this pulse by 'walking on the spot', beginning on the right foot. This is not a four-four beat; it's just a pulse, with no accent or subdivision. Keep it steady, don't race. Keep listening to the metronome and walking the pulse. If you feel the metronome is dragging you or rushing you, adjust your speed to match the metronome speed. Later we will internalise the pulse, but for now it's in the feet while we continue to work on unified pulse.

Feet: right left right left etc. ———————→

VARIATION: A TEMPO CHANGE

Appoint a leader to stand in the centre of the circle to lead changes in the speed of the pulse from slow to medium to fast, by simply changing walking speed and everyone following. Try sudden and gradual changes. Swap and give others a turn at leading the tempo change.

CONDUCTING PATTERN

A basic four-four conducting pattern is an example of a unified pulse. Here is a diagram of the conducting pattern viewed from the conductor's side.

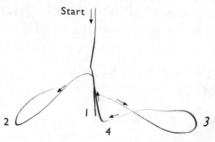

Introduce the conducting pattern and ask everyone to try it out and get used to waving their arms around. Invite a conductor to lead the group once more to indicate tempo changes, but this time using the conducting patterns. Is this easier to follow than watching someone's feet?

CHAPTER 15:
METRE EXERCISES

Pulse can be grouped into twos, threes or fours etc.
Groups of pulses constitute musical metre.

UNIFIED PULSE AND METRE

Step the following patterns in the feet with a metronome
sounding. Begin on the right foot and emphasise the first
pulse in sets of two (by playing it a little bit louder),
then three, then four, then five, then six, then seven,
then eight, and then nine. Note that the first pulse
changes from right foot to left foot in the odd metres.
The group leader calls the changes. Keep the tempo
steady at 60 b.p.m.

Feet: Right, left, right, left, right, left etc.

Speed = 60 b.p.m.

R   L   R   L   R   L   R . L etc

Grouped in twos

R L R L R L R L R L R L R L R L

Grouped in threes

```
R   L   R | L   R   L | R   L   R | L   R   L | R   L   R  ──→
```

Grouped in fours

```
R   L   R   L | R   L   R   L | R   L   R   L | R   L   R   L  ──→
```

Grouped in fives

```
R   L   R   L   R | L   R   L   R   L | R   L   R   L   R  ──→
```

Grouped in sixes

```
R   L   R   L   R   L | R   L   R   L   R   L  ──→
```

Grouped in sevens

```
R   L   R   L   R   L   R | L   R   L   R   L   R   L  ──→
```

ADD A CLAP

Repeat the above with the leader sounding the pulse
(use claves or a cowbell) and the players clapping on
the first of each grouping (keeping the feet still), for
example in threes:

```
            clap
Group:  x⤸       x        x        x        x        etc.
Leader: ♩  ♩  ♩  ♩  ♩  ♩  ♩  ♩  ♩  ♩  ♩  ♩  ♩  ♩  ♩  ──→
```

In fours

Group: x   x   x   x   etc.
Leader: • • • • • • • • • • • • • • • • ⟶

In fives

Group: x   x   x   etc.
Leader: • • • • • • • • • • • • • • • • ⟶

UNIFIED PULSE AND INDEPENDENT METRE

THREE AND FOUR

Split the circle and ask one half to clap the first of a three-pulse metre and the other half to clap the first of a four-pulse metre. Count four to begin. Twelve beats will go by before the group plays a 'one' together again.

Group A: x   x   x   ⌐   x   etc.
Leader: • • • • • • • • • • • • • • • ⟶
Group B: x   x   x   x

THREE AND FIVE

How many before a unified 'one'?

Group A: x   x   x   x   x   etc.
Leader: • • • • • • • • • • • • • • • ⟶
Group B: x   x   x

THREE, FOUR AND FIVE

This will take a cycle of 60 pulses to return to a unified 'one'.

Group A: x   x   x
Group B: x   x   x   x
Group C: x   x   x   x   x
Leader: • • • • • • • • • • • • • • • ⟶   etc.

VARIATION 1: VOCAL VERSION

Replace the clap with a vocal sound. Assign high, medium and low registers to the groups. Ask each to quickly decide on a sound or word, to be performed in the allocated register. The sound should have a percussive attack quality to help articulate the resultant rhythm. Count to four then begin.

VARIATION 2: VOCAL AND MOVEMENT VERSION

Each group adds a stepping movement to their sound. Try to recognise the end of the cycle by listening for the unified 'one' and stopping/freezing. Try starting each group in different places and use different directions across the space, from upstage to downstage in a line and vice versa, using directed walking patterns or any other variations the group suggests. Always count to four then begin.

PERFORMANCE TASK

In smaller groups, combine, summarise and resolve the above exercises into a short (5 minute) performance, which clearly demonstrates and changes between:
▶ independent pulse;
▶ unified pulse;
▶ unified pulse and metre;
▶ unified pulse and independent metre.
Incorporate tempo changes into the piece.

CHAPTER 16: RHYTHM EXERCISES

THE RHYTHM–PULSE RELATIONSHIP

The placement of sounds in relation to pulse creates rhythm.

Demonstrate rhythm with 'Mary Had a Little Lamb'. The group can mark the pulse by stamping feet and clapping the rhythm of the words.

Clap the rhythm only:

Mar-y   had a   lit-tle lamb,   lit-tle lamb,   lit-tle lamb.

The feet show the pulse, which is usually internal or silent, and the hands show the rhythm. The two are related to each other and combine to give rhythm meaning. This may seem obvious but even quite accomplished players might not have thought about it before. Rhythm is always in relationship to pulse. Rhythm without pulse has no meaning even if the pulse is irregular or random.

Here is a more sophisticated example to demonstrate the rhythm/pulse relationship:

No pulse—clap as loop:

In 12/8:

Pulse

In 3/2:

Pulse

DISCUSSION TOPICS
▶ What examples of experiencing pulse in relation to rhythm can you recall?
▶ Have you ever realised after some time that you were listening with an incorrect or misconceived pulse?
▶ Is it necessary for the audience to experience an inner pulse in order to appreciate rhythm?

ON-BEATS AND OFF-BEATS
VARIATION 1
Again using the rhythm of 'Mary Had a Little Lamb', leave out the beats that coincide with the pulse, leaving only the off-beats. Place a strong pulse in the feet:

Clap the off-beats only:

Graeme Leak
PERFORMANCE MAKING

VARIATION 2

With the pulse in the feet, clap four beats 'on' and four beats 'off' the pulse. Notice the feeling and the direction of the movement in the second bar as you spring off the beat:

Now reverse the second bar, putting the pulse in the hands and the off-beat in the feet. Notice the difference in the feeling and direction of the movement.

Finally combine both in a three-bar pattern. Work slowly at first until the co-ordination settles:

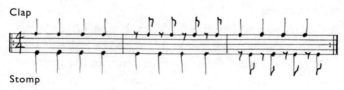

PERFORMANCE TASK

In smaller groups, stamp the feet in unison to create a pulse. Improvise clapping patterns that clearly are either on or off the pulse beats. Work with the idea for a while until an interesting collective/combined rhythm is created.

Make the external pulse disappear and become internal (use some small movements to stay in sync with others). Transfer the clapping improvisations to instruments and/or voices and/or percussion. Find ways to make an interesting 3–5 minute performance and present it to the class.

RHYTHM CIRCLE
ESTABLISHING THE PHRASE LENGTH

Stand in a circle and establish a unison pulse (about 60 b.p.m.) in the feet that is gentle and not too loud (it is best to take your shoes off). Aim for perfect unison. Feel the pulse strongly. Use your whole body, with the pulse being firmly grounded.

Emphasise the first of every four pulses—a unison metre of four.

Grouped in fours

Add a vocal 'hey' on the first of every four bars:

'Hey!'

Play for a while until this phrase of four bars feels easy and natural. Then try the rhythm circle.

Each player invents a combination of on-beats and off-beats over four pulses to make a rhythm. This rhythm is 'your own'. To find 'your own' rhythm, take one step back (widening the circle) and explore different combinations until you find the one you like. When you are happy, step forward and keep playing 'your own'. When everyone has stepped forward we are ready to play (at this point the room is filled with individual rhythms sounding together). The leader instructs each player to play 'their own' rhythm for four bars. During the sixteen pulses, the leader identifies the first soloist. When the leader shouts 'hey', the group stops. The first soloist then plays his or her pattern for one bar (call), then the group copies it for three bars (response).

The players then play 'their own' rhythm for four bars (16 pulses), and during this time, the leader identifies the next soloist.

The second soloist plays his or her pattern alone for one bar (call), and the group copies it for three bars (response).

And so on around the circle (or across the circle in any order ... surprises are good).

On an individual level this form translates to: 'I play "my own" rhythm for four bars, I listen to someone else's for one bar and copy it for three bars, then I play "my own" rhythm again for four bars.'

This is a good activity for both first time and experienced groups.

SUBDIVISION OF PULSE

Once a unified sense of pulse has been established and practised, it can be subdivided. Begin with twos, threes and fours—fives, sixes and sevens etc. can come later.

With a strong unison pulse in the feet, clap the following subdivisions. When practising, notice how the subdivisions relate to the pulse (especially the off-beat triplets and semiquavers).

In twos (quavers):

In threes (triplets):

In fours (semiquavers):

SUBDIVISION RHYTHM CIRCLE

After practising subdivision in twos, threes and fours, perform the rhythm circle using specific subdivisions as the basis for 'your own' rhythm. For example, give an instruction like, 'during today's rhythm circle we are going to use only triplets'.

PERFORMANCE TASKS

An awareness of pulse, rhythm and metre permeates all of the performances after the concepts have been introduced. Specific tasks can be set after the introduction of each exercise. Even an instruction such as 'make a piece which refers to the rhythm work just done' will generate an interesting variety of responses.

GROUPING PULSES IN TWOS AND THREES

As noted earlier, our time-keeping machines have influenced Western music traditions. Most musical time is based on a prescribed pulse at a certain speed with rhythms as subdivisions of that pulse.

Another approach is to take a faster pulse, and group that pulse in mixes of twos and threes. For clarity, the following examples show groupings of twelve pulses; however this can be any number you choose. The triangle represents a group of three and the slash, a group of two. Clap the first in each group while the leader sounds the rapid pulse. You can then use the triangle/slash as shorthand to quickly devise rhythmic schemes based on all kinds of numbers.

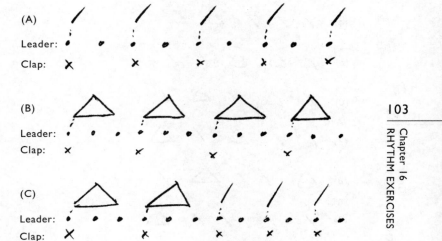

A shorthand version of the above would look like:

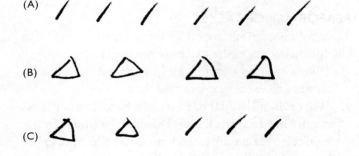

Try these. Use (A) or (B) or (C) as a regular pulse against which to sound the following examples:

(4)   / / / △ △

(5)   / △ △ / /

(6)   / △ / △ /

(7)   / / △ / △

(8)   △ / / △ /

(9)   / △ / / △

(10) △ / △ / /

PERFORMANCE TASKS

The above groupings are on a base number of twelve. In the following examples the base number changes.

(1) Divide into two groups and assign a different base number to each. Perform together.

(2) Ask each individual to think of a base number. This results in a beautiful, ever-changing rhythmic fabric held together not by a common metre (grouping) but by a common pulse. It helps if the leader sounds the pulse on a clave or a cowbell at first.

(3) Think of any even number between eight and twenty four. This becomes the group's base number. Devise a scheme of grouping based on twos and threes, using the shorthand of triangles and slashes, as above. Develop a performance of these rhythms:

▶ with voice and body percussion only;
▶ with instruments only (use any pitch—just worry about making the rhythms accurate);
▶ mixed instruments, voices and percussion.

CHAPTER 17: TONE EXERCISES

TONE

A tone is a musical note of a particular frequency.

FIND THE NOTE

Imagine a tone. Imagine hearing it clearly, but don't sing it out loud yet. On cue we'll all sing our note loudly and confidently. The result should be a cluster of unrelated tones all sounding at once.

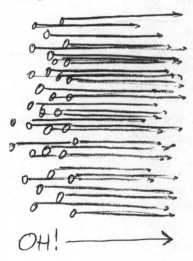

OH! ⟶

Keep singing your note, taking breaths as necessary. Begin to wander around the room, listening to other notes from other singers as you go. Keep singing. Don't let the note die; make it louder, louder and more confident. Hold on to your note and don't be influenced by what you hear.

Now stop moving (but keep singing) as you encounter another singer and listen specifically to his or her note. Sing into each other's ears so you can focus on each other's note. Decide whether the other note you are hearing is higher or lower than yours, and negotiate unison. This means that both singers adjust their notes to arrive at the same one. So if my note is higher, I slide my note down while my partner slides up and we should arrive at the same note. It is better for males to sing to males and females to sing to females to avoid confusion with register. When you and your partner find the same note, walk away and find a new partner and repeat the process.

Duo finds unison:

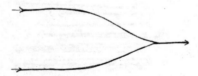

The process continues. Gradually the room becomes less dissonant and more consonant.

Ensemble thins out to consonance:

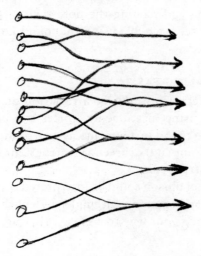

With persistence and the ability to 'let go' of what you had and sing something new, eventually the group arrives at 'the note'. Build its strength and power, and conduct a cut-off at a climactic point.

Group arrives at unison note:

NAME THE NOTE

Put forward nominations on which note it is, and take votes. Anyone is free to nominate the name of the pitch. Is it a C♯ or a G? Use the piano to reveal the true identity of the note. Congratulate the winners.

TONES AND SEMITONES

After finding and naming the note revisit 'Tones and semitones' (see page 80) using the found note instead of A.

PERFORMANCE TASK

(1) In smaller groups, devise a variation on the above exercise using instruments, voices and percussion. Try using found instruments as well as making your own. See appendix three for instructions on how to make a string can.

(2) The idea of unison could be interpreted rhythmically, perhaps all beginning with independent rhythms and negotiating your way to a unison rhythm.

CHAPTER 18: MELODY AND HARMONY EXERCISES

MELODY AND HARMONY

Harmony in music is the result of a group of tones sounding simultaneously. A melody is a sequence of particular tones, and it is distinct from harmony and rhythm. (For more details, see the glossary.)

I always remember the words of the composer Carl Vine whom I was fortunate to work with in the 1980s. He said to me one day, 'Graeme, I've finally figured out the secret to harmony. Trust your ears'. We all have a unique ability to decide what sounds good to us. If you trust this instinct, your music will sound good to you and (chances are) to others, too. (If it doesn't, they'll just have to get used to it!)

The following exercises ask the performers to listen and trust the ear.

CONSONANCE AND DISSONANCE

Following on from our work with tones and semitones, and assuming that we are all able to accurately sing up a scale one semitone at a time, we can now explore a range of intervals (two notes sounding at the same time).

Split the group into pairs and scatter around the room. Find a low unison note and sing it together. (It is best to have males paired with males and females with females for true unison in the same register.) One singer stays on that note and the other sings up the scale, one semitone at a time. The duo makes notes at each step along the way. What does it sound like with two notes a semitone apart or two semitones apart? Name each interval according to their distance apart in semitones. Give each interval a rating on a scale from tense to relaxed. Which is the most tense? Which is the most calm, stable and relaxed?

PERFORMANCE TASK
Ask each duo to prepare a piece demonstrating an order of intervals from calm to tense, or vice versa. Discuss and compare.

UNISON
Ask a participant to help you demonstrate the following. One leads, the other follows, and both remain in perfect unison. Sing slow-moving melodies at first that don't leap around too much, and then try to trick your partner with some surprises. It's quite easy to do and effective for the listener—with practice, improvised unison-duo singing sounds quite rehearsed and organised.

Split into a collection of pairs around the room and all practice unison-duo singing. Swap the roles of leader and follower.

Bring all the pairs back together in a circle and perform a piece with individual unison-duos sounding in parallel with each other. Listen to the whole piece and float through a range of consonant and dissonant periods. Try to finish on a consonant, relaxed chord.

PERFORMANCE TASKS

(1) GROUP IMPROVISATION

Form a large group in a circle, sing long, sustained notes and listen to the degree of consonance and dissonance in the resulting chords. Change notes slowly—with each new breath perhaps. Make changes in pitch in small steps only. Insert silences between notes. Listen at all times. Try as a group to keep the piece alive and interesting. Use variations with dynamics and timbre. Explore for at least 10 minutes. Record and listen back.

(2) ADD A MELODY

Repeat the improvisation and this time, if you hear a melody that could float over the harmonic changes, sing it or play it on your instrument. Explore multiple melodies. At what point do individual notes become a melody and how?

CHAPTER 19:
TIMBRE EXERCISES

TIMBRE

Timbre is the colour of a musical sound. Each sound is comprised of a mixture of sounds, the lowest tone being the fundamental tone and the overtones being any tones higher in frequency than the fundamental one. The overtones present in a sound create timbre, and they also give distinguishing characteristics to the sounds created by different instruments.

Instrumentalists and singers aspire to a sound colour that is acceptable in a certain style context. For example, classical players might prefer a rich, pure and full tone while jazz players might like a more individual and expressive tone colour. Something often overlooked is the possibility of virtually unlimited variations in tone colour. The following exercises use word and colour associations to get the group thinking visually and exploring new possibilities in tone colour.

RESPONSES TO COLOUR
EXERCISE 1

Ask participants to list some words that they associate with the following colours:

▶ red;
▶ yellow;

- blue;
- orange;
- purple;
- pink;
- dark green, and any other colour.

On a whiteboard list the words that were common to particular colours. Compare the lists and discuss. Does there appear to be a common language in relation to colour association?

EXERCISE 2

As a large ensemble, improvise short pieces in response to the original list of colour words, firstly using only voices and body percussion and then with instruments, voices and percussion. Do lots of short (1–2 minute) pieces and keep the pace up.

EXERCISE 3: MORE TRIGGER WORDS

Demonstrate with your voice a sound that changes slowly from 'fat'/'breathy' (think of Elvis Presley's voice) to 'thin'/'tight' (think of Bob Dylan's voice). Pass around a single note in a circle and ask each person to change the colour of the note before passing it on.

List words on a whiteboard to describe the sounds just made. The list may look something like this:
- cool;
- warm;
- breathy;
- tight;
- light;
- fat;
- thick;
- thin;
- dry;
- nasal;
- dark.

Workshop the list and sort it into contrasting pairs, such as:
- ▶ thick/thin;
- ▶ cool/warm;
- ▶ breathy/nasal.

PERFORMANCE TASK

Assign a word pair each to smaller groups and ask for a piece which demonstrates movement from the first word to the second word or vice versa, with variations. Some structural possibilities, for example, from 'thin' to 'thick' include:

Unison: everyone performs from 'thin' to 'thick':

Reverse: everyone performs from 'thick' to 'thin':

Overlap: the group divides in half to perform a cross fade:

Changes are random (slow/medium/fast):

EXPLORATORY FOLLOW-UP

Try experimenting with timbre individually on instruments and voice. Ask:

▶ How would you describe your normal tone colour?
▶ How many ways can you think of to change that colour?
▶ What is the most unmusical tone colour you can make?
▶ What is the thinnest?
▶ What is the fattest?
▶ What is the driest?
▶ What is the wettest?
▶ What is the harshest?
▶ What is the smoothest?

Participants might like to report back to the group with any discoveries that they have made.

CHAPTER 20: DYNAMICS EXERCISES

DYNAMIC LEVELS

The dynamic range of a sound is the range in its volume or intensity.

EXERCISE

Say the number 'one' on the first beat of a four-four bar as softly as you possibly can. Rehearse with a conductor, perform and discuss. Is that really the softest you can say it? Where is the border between audible and inaudible? Is it possible to say it so softly that not everyone in the room hears you? Add the number 'two' on the second beat in your loudest possible voice. Rehearse with a conductor, perform and discuss.

Does loud necessarily mean ugly and harsh? Can it be a really loud yet really beautiful sound? Does register (high/low) have anything to do with your perception of loudness? That is, do higher sounds seem louder and vice versa?

Introduce the number 'three'. Now 'one' is the softest, 'two' is exactly half way between 'one' and 'three' and 'three' is the loudest. Rehearse and perform. Split the group in two. Let one half perform, while the other half listens then provides critical feedback on ways to improve the performance. Swap.

Add more levels of dynamic to the piece until you reach 'ten'. Notice the difficulty in performing the more subtle shades. Notice the tendency to drop too suddenly from loudest to second loudest. Ask for ideas on variation. Try using instruments for one version.

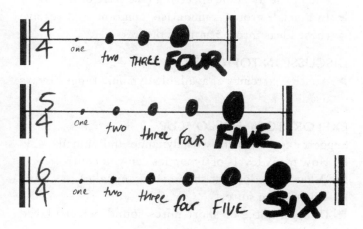

Assuming a dynamic range of one to ten, write up sequences of numbers in any order and perform them as dynamic pieces, for example:

▶ 1 3 2 5 6 4 1 2 3 5 9 10;
▶ 3 5 7 9 10 8 6 4 2 1;
▶ 1 10 2 9 3 8 4 7 5 6 5 4 3 2 1.

Try this five-part dynamic piece. 'One' is the softest possible, 'five' is the loudest.

Group one provides the pulse. Add other groups one at a time.

PERFORMANCE TASKS

▶ Transfer the above pieces to instruments and voices. Rehearse and perform.

▶ Ask groups to invent variations along similar ideas to explore dynamic range.

▶ Revisit the exercises on silence that explore the soft end of the dynamic spectrum (see page 87).

▶ In a small group, summarise, combine and resolve these ideas into a 5-minute piece.

DISCUSSION TOPICS

▶ Are the extremes of available dynamic range always used?

EXPLORATORY FOLLOW-UP

Suggest experimenting with dynamics individually. Ask:

▶ How many levels of dynamics can you control?

▶ What is the loudest sound you can make?

▶ What is the softest?

▶ Do long notes or short notes sound better played loudly?

▶ Do long notes or short notes sound better played softly?

▶ How many different ways can you change from one dynamic to the other (for example, slowly or suddenly)? How else?

CHAPTER 21: TEXTURE EXERCISES

TEXTURE

The texture of a piece of music is the relationship between independent sounds occurring together at any one time in the music.

EXERCISE 1

Form a circle, then launch into the following exercise. Keep talking until the group catches on to what you are doing and begins to join in one at a time. Start by saying:

'I am talking now about texture and density. You are listening to the sound of my voice only—a sparse, thin texture. Gradually to my left, others will enter one at a time and we will hear the effects of additional voices as the texture changes from sparse to dense. I just have to keep going with this nonsense now because I can't stop until the texture builds up to everyone in the room talking. This morning I went for a short bike ride to pump up my tyres but the air at the garage was out of order so I had to cycle for miles to the next garage and on the way there I got a puncture and had to walk home', and so on.

As the group gets the idea and the sound level increases, yell the following:

'To be heard over the dense texture you can try using a louder dynamic or a higher pitch or both. You could also try a much lower pitch (register). If the bulk of sound is in a particular register, then sounding lower or higher will get you through a dense texture.'

EXERCISE 2

'This time when I talk ...... about texture and density I am going to ...... insert some long gaps so that ...... the ratio of sound to silence ...... is about 50:50 ...... Let's do what we did ...... last time and each voice enters ...... one at a time with the same ...... long gaps and we'll observe ...... the difference in the overall texture ......' etc.

Sound recordists and composers think a lot about register in relation to density. A satisfying mix is achieved when voices and instruments with a variety of registers are combined together.

VARIATIONS

▶ Start and stop the exercise, while the solo voice continues.

▶ List descriptive words, for example:

    ▶ thick/thin (this also applies to timbre);

    ▶ dense/sparse;

    ▶ rough/smooth.

▶ Illustrate graphically.

PERFORMANCE TASK

Make a piece about texture in music. Demonstrate the idea of moving from sparse to dense (or vice versa) and include moments where a solo voice is either masked by the texture or manages to cut through.

Notate or illustrate this piece to allow others to interpret it.

CHAPTER 22: DURATION EXERCISES

DURATION

All sounds and silences have duration. They can be short, medium, long or anywhere in between.

Some work was done on silence/sound ratios in the section on silence on page 87.

EXERCISES

In a circle, ask for short improvisations (1–2 minutes) in response to the following instructions. Use voices, body percussion or instruments in any combination. Players should focus solely on how long their sound is, and how long their rests are:

▶ very short sounds and very long silences;
▶ very long sounds and very long silences;
▶ very long sounds and very short silences;
▶ short sounds and short silences;
▶ sounds change slowly from short to long and silences do the same;
▶ the reverse of the last instruction;
▶ medium length sounds and medium length silences;
▶ random/free choice: listen and make the piece interesting.

PERFORMANCE TASK

In smaller groups discuss the pieces just improvised. Predetermine a duration scheme for a 4-minute piece. Rehearse, refine and present your piece to the rest of the class.

APPENDIX I:
COURSE PLANS

ONE-SESSION COURSE PLAN
2 hours

1. STRETCHES/ WARM-UP —20 minutes	In any order: ▶ floor stretches (9)–(12), p 44. ▶ standing stretches (2), (4) and (9), p 51. ▶ send the clap around/send the sound around: p 68.
2. GAMES —15 minutes	▶ Ball name game: p 70. ▶ Barrier name game: p 71.
3. DISCUSS/ LISTEN —10 minutes	▶ Discuss the nature of the session and what is going to happen. Refer to the performance-making principles.
4. FOCUS ON —30 minutes	Pitch: ▶ find the note: p 105. ▶ name the note: p 107. ▶ sing major, minor, diminished and augmented chords: p 82. Rhythm: ▶ define pulse and metre: pp 77 and 92. ▶ demonstrate independent pulse/no metre: p 89; ▶ demonstrate unified pulse/unified metre: p 92; ▶ demonstrate unified pulse/independent metre: p 94.

5. BREAK —10 minutes	
6. PERFORM-ANCE TASKS —20 minutes	In small groups, make a piece that includes: ▶ some independent pulse; ▶ some unified pulse; ▶ some unified metre; ▶ a chord progression with at least two of the chords featured earlier.
7. PERFORM-ANCES —10 minutes	▶ Make notes on the performances of each group.
8. FEEDBACK — 5 minutes	▶ Make notes about the discussion and guide and assist the feedback process.

THREE-SESSION COURSE PLAN

3 x 2 hour sessions

SESSION 1	
1. STRETCHES /WARM-UP —20 minutes	▶ Isolation exercises: p 39. ▶ Sing musical rounds: p 69.
2. GAMES —15 minutes	▶ Ball name games: p 70. ▶ Ball game '50 Up': p 72.
3. DISCUSS/ LISTEN —10 minutes	▶ Present an overview of topics and discuss. ▶ Exercise: A walk outside: p 62.
4. FOCUS ON —30 minutes	▶ Music skill: Pulse = 60 b.p.m.: p 77. ▶ Noise exercises: p 85. ▶ Silence exercises: p 87. ▶ Dynamics exercises: p 116.
5. BREAK —10 minutes	

6. PERFORM-ANCE TASKS —20 minutes	▶ Make pieces that refer to noise, silence and dynamics. ▶ Perform with an awareness of the environmental sounds heard in a walk outside.
7. PERFORM-ANCES —10 minutes	▶ Record the performances for replay at the next session. ▶ Make notes on group members and group dynamics.
8. FEEDBACK —5 minutes	▶ Make notes about the discussion.

SESSION 2

1. STRETCHES /WARM-UP —20 minutes	▶ Some floor and standing stretches: pp 44 and 51. ▶ Directed walking: p 66.
2. GAMES —15 minutes	▶ Tippity: p 71.
3. DISCUSS/ LISTEN —10 minutes	▶ Play tape of last session's performances. ▶ Discuss.
4. FOCUS ON —30 minutes	▶ Music skill: A = 440 c.p.s.: p 79. ▶ Timbre exercises: p 112. ▶ Texture exercises: p 119. ▶ Duration exercises: p 121.
5. BREAK —10 minutes	
6. PERFORM-ANCE TASKS —20 minutes	▶ Devise pieces which utilise all of the workspace and refer to timbre, texture, duration and directed walking.
7. PERFORM-ANCES —10 minutes	▶ Each group is to perform their piece. ▶ Ask the audience to consider elements for possible use in the final performances in session three.

8. FEEDBACK —5 minutes	▶ Consider the material from sessions one and two which should be focused on in session three.

SESSION 3

1. STRETCHES /WARM-UP— 20 minutes	▶ Some floor and standing stretches: pp 44 and 51. ▶ Directed walking: p 66.
2. GAMES —15 minutes	▶ British bulldog: p 72.
3. DISCUSS/ LISTEN —10 minutes	▶ Present a plan for combining performances from sessions one and two into a piece to be performed in this session.
4. BREAK —10 minutes	
5. PERFORM- ANCE TASKS —30 minutes	▶ Work as a large group to create a combined showing of the work generated in sessions one and two.
6. PERFORM- ANCES —20 minutes	▶ Perform and record the piece.
7. FEEDBACK —15 minutes	▶ Play back the tape and discuss.

TEN-SESSION COURSE PLAN

10 x 2 hour sessions

	SESSION 1	SESSION 2
1. STRETCHES /WARM-UP— 20 minutes	▶ Isolation exercises: p 39.	▶ Floor and standing stretches: pp 44 and 51.
2. GAMES —15 minutes	▶ Stand there and do nothing: p 64. ▶ Name games: p 70.	▶ Tippity: p 71.
3. DISCUSS/ LISTEN —10 minutes	▶ Outline the course.	▶ A walk outside: p 62.
4. FOCUS ON —30 minutes	Music skills: ▶ Pulse = 60 b.p.m.: p 77. ▶ Noise: p 85.	Music skills: ▶ A = 440 c.p.s.: p 79. ▶ Silence: p 87.
5. BREAK —10 minutes		
6. PERFORM-ANCE TASKS —20 minutes	▶ Explore the noise performance task: p 86. ▶ Refer to music skills: p 77. ▶ Use a 60 b.p.m. pulse in the piece.	▶ Explore silence performance task: p 88. ▶ Refer to listening exercises and music skills: pp 62 and 77. ▶ Sing an A in the piece.
7. PERFORM-ANCES —10 minutes	▶ Record the performances. ▶ Note the group members' names.	▶ Record the performances. ▶ Note the group members' names.
8. FEEDBACK —5 minutes	▶ Plan for the session six performance.	▶ Discuss the performances.

	SESSION 3	SESSION 4
1. STRETCHES /WARM-UP— 20 minutes	▶ Floor and standing stretches: pp 44 and 51. ▶ Directed walking: p 66.	▶ Floor and standing stretches: pp 44 and 51. ▶ Directed walking: p 66.
2. GAMES —15 minutes	▶ Tell stories a word at a time: p 73.	▶ Statues: p 74. ▶ Make a picture: p 74.
3. DISCUSS/ LISTEN —10 minutes	▶ Listen to and discuss the tapes of performances.	▶ Discuss the material for the session six performance.
4. FOCUS ON —30 minutes	Music skills: ▶ Tones and semitones: p 80. ▶ Pulse: p 89.	Music skills: ▶ Triads: p 82.
5. BREAK —10 minutes		
6. PERFORM-ANCE TASKS —20 minutes	▶ Explore the tones and semitones performance task: p 80. ▶ Refer to music skills and pulse: pp 77 and 89.	▶ Explore the triads performance task: p 82.
7. PERFORM-ANCES —10 minutes	▶ Record the performances. ▶ Note the group members' names.	▶ Record the performances. ▶ Note the group members' names.
8. FEEDBACK —5 minutes	▶ Discuss which pieces to use in the session six performance.	▶ Discuss the performances.

	SESSION 5	SESSION 6
1. STRETCHES /WARM-UP— 20 minutes	▶ Floor and standing stretches: pp 44 and 51. ▶ Rhythm circle: p 99.	▶ Warm up: p 62.
2. GAMES —15 minutes	▶ Name-writing dance: p 76.	
3. DISCUSS/ LISTEN —10 minutes	▶ Finalise material for the session six performance.	
4. FOCUS ON —30 minutes	▶ Rehearse material from the first four sessions and plan for the session six performance.	
5. BREAK —10 minutes		
6. PERFORM- ANCE TASKS —20 minutes	▶ Continue to rehearse for the session six performance.	▶ Perform several dress rehearsals.
7. PERFORM- ANCES —10 minutes	▶ Record the performances. ▶ Note the group members' names.	▶ Present a performance for family and friends. ▶ Record the performance.
8. FEEDBACK —5 minutes	▶ Discuss the performances.	▶ Debrief.

	SESSION 7	SESSION 8
1. STRETCHES /WARM-UP— 20 minutes	▶ Floor and standing stretches: pp 44 and 51. ▶ Rhythm circle: p 99.	▶ Floor and standing stretches: pp 44 and 51. ▶ Sing musical rounds: p 69. OR ▶ Move straight into performance rehearsals.
2. GAMES —15 minutes	▶ Status games: p 72.	
3. DISCUSS/ LISTEN —10 minutes	▶ Listen to the tape of the session six performance and discuss.	
4. FOCUS ON —30 minutes	▶ Melody and harmony: p 109. OR ▶ Metre: p 92.	▶ Timbre: p 112. OR ▶ Dynamics: p 116. OR ▶ Duration: p 121.
5. BREAK —10 minutes		
6. PERFORM- ANCE TASKS —20 minutes 7. PERFORM- ANCES —10 minutes 8. FEEDBACK —5 minutes	▶ Focus performance tasks on the final show. New skills may be introduced as performance pieces are re-worked, shaped and rehearsed for the final show.	▶ Focus performance tasks on the final show. New skills may be introduced as performance pieces are re-worked, shaped and rehearsed for the final show.

	SESSION 9	SESSION 10
1. STRETCHES /WARM-UP	▶ Floor and standing stretches: pp 44 and 51.	▶ Floor and standing stretches: pp 44 and 51. ▶ Directed walking: p 66. ▶ Tones and semitones: p 80.
2. REHEARSALS	▶ Final rehearsal, re-working and shaping of performance piece.	▶ Open the rooms and let the audience in.
3. PERFORM-ANCES	▶ Run through dress rehearsal at least twice.	▶ Perform with ease, confidence and power. ▶ Record the performance.
4. FEEDBACK	▶ Ensure that everyone is clear about their role in the show.	▶ Debrief. ▶ Perhaps meet socially at a later date to listen to the tape of the performance or watch the video, and discuss.

APPENDIX 2: MAKING A PERFORMANCE

This appendix features draft and final running orders from a production called 'Happy New Ears', performed by the IHOS Opera in 2001. The running orders demonstrate the process of making a performance out of material generated during a performance-making workshop.

Based in Hobart, the IHOS Opera mounts professional large-scale dramatic/musical productions. The IHOS Music Theatre Laboratory also trains young performers in vocal and dramatic techniques, and guest directors work with groups in training sessions to develop public performances.

'Happy New Ears' was developed with the author as guest director in May 2001 during a series of workshops over a two-week period. The workshop material used is largely contained in this book. Out of exercises exploring rhythm, pulse, tone, dynamics, texture and timbre, the performers created small group pieces and these were assembled into a 30-minute piece. The working titles of each piece became the running order as shown overleaf.

recounted to me. Unable to afford clarinets for his year seven music classes, the teacher was, however, able to purchase twenty-five mouthpieces. He attached these to lengths of PVC pipe with holes drilled to create recorder-like instruments. After a few sessions with these instruments, the students learnt how to produce a sound with an embouchure. Those students who showed interest and ability were then given the opportunity to graduate to a real instrument when they entered the band program in year eight.

In the Music Department at La Trobe University, there was an 'Improv Lab', which had been established in the 1970s by Professor Keith Humble and Dr Jeff Pressing. Many music students utilised the lab's collection of junk and found instruments as they explored the processes of composing and performing. During my decade at La Trobe from 1990 to 1999, I added to the collection, mainly with an assortment of metal storage drums. This became known as the 'Noise Orchestra' and it formed the centrepiece of several ensembles.

On the following page are instructions for building an instrument which I call the 'string can'. It is based on the ancient model of a single string, a stick and a resonator—the earliest known example of which is the hunter's bow. In effect, this instrument is the ancestor of the modern string family.

For further reading, see *Musical Instrument Design* by Bart Hopkin (See Sharp Press, Tucson, Arizona 1996).

HOW TO MAKE A STRING CAN

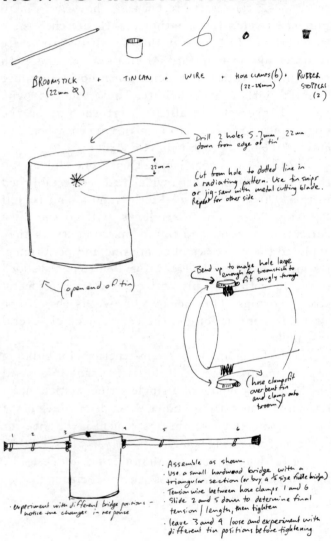

BROOMSTICK
(22mm ⌀) + TIN CAN + WIRE + HOSE CLAMPS (6) + RUBBER
(22-28mm) STOPPERS
(2)

Drill 2 holes 5.7mm, 22mm
down from edge of tin'

22mm

Cut from hole to dotted line in
a radiating pattern. Use tin snips
or jig-saw with metal cutting blade.
Repeat for other side.

← (open end of tin)

Bend up to make hole large
enough for broomstick to
fit snugly through

(hose clamps fit
over bent tin
and clamp onto
broom)

1   2   3   4   5   6

· experiment with different bridge positions -
notice the changes in response

· Assemble as shown.
· Use a small hardwood bridge with a
triangular section (or buy a ½ size fiddle bridge)
· Tension wire between hose clamps 1 and 6
· Slide 2 and 5 down to determine final
tension / length, then tighten
· leave 3 and 4 loose and experiment with
different tin positions before tightening

APPENDIX 4: GLOSSARY

The following definitions are useful in the context of this book but they are not intended to be universal definitions of the terms.

ATTACK

As a sound occurs it moves through four main phases: attack, decay, sustain and release. The attack of a sound encompasses the time it takes to reach its peak. The characteristics of a sound in the first few milliseconds therefore make up its attack. Sounds created by bowed instruments (such as violins) generally have slow, non-percussive attacks; it is as if the sounds 'sneak in'. Sounds from percussion instruments (such as xylophones or snare drums) usually have very rapid attacks. Wind players can choose to play sharp, quick attacks or slower, smoother notes.

CLOSE POSITION

A close position chord has notes which are as close together as possible.

CONSONANCE AND DISSONANCE

A listener's subjective reaction to combinations of sounds can range from consonance to dissonance. In general, consonant sounds are pleasing to the ear, whereas dissonant sounds are jarring. Historically, Western audiences have found jarring sounds in music to be challenging. Beethoven was booed resoundingly for his use of dissonant sounds. Even early Beatles fans were appalled at their later releases. Some listeners are still shocked by the music of Arnold Schoenberg (1874–1951) nearly one hundred years after he invented new rules for harmony. Some experiments have shown that repeated exposure to dissonant sounds can lead to the listener responding with acceptance and even pleasure.

DOWNSTAGE AND UPSTAGE

Upstage and downstage are directions to help performers remember their positions on stage ... Think of the stage as a slope. When you walk away from the audience towards the back wall, you walk upstage. When you walk towards the audience, you travel downstage. Hence when a downstage performer is unaware of the antics of a performer who is located behind and is attracting the audience's attention, she or he is being upstaged.

DURATION

Duration is the amount of time a sound or an event lasts. Performance events usually give a clear indication to the audience when they have started and when they stop. Composers think a lot about duration in relation to different instruments. Some instruments are good at playing notes with a long duration while others are not. Sounds with the longest duration are created using instruments that can be played with circular breathing like the didjeridu and the trombone.

TIMBRE

Timbre is the colour of a musical sound and it is primarily determined by the overtones present in the sound (see overtones). Instrumental performers can vary the colour of their sounds with a range of techniques. Violinists can play closer to the bridge, or pluck with the fingers. Percussionists can use hard or soft mallets. Guitars can be altered by a myriad of combinations of effects, tone controls and amplifiers. Voices can be dark and breathy, or nasal and thin.

TONE

A tone is a musical note of a particular frequency. If we sing our lowest note and then slide up the scale to our highest, we've just performed every tone available in our range. If we decide to move in steps instead of a smooth line, we are probably using a combination of tones and semitones.

TONES AND SEMITONES

The Western tuning system divides the musical range into steps and half-steps, that is, tones and semitones. We have, over time, arbitrarily determined that certain frequencies are called octaves and that there are twelve steps in each octave. In this sense, the tone is a whole step while a semitone is a half-step.

On the piano keyboard the distance between any two notes adjacent to each other, black or white, is a semitone.

Other tuning systems are used in music from different parts of the world. When we hear music using a different tuning system than the one to which we are accustomed, we automatically tend to judge it as 'out of tune'. What we think of as 'in' and 'out' of tune is entirely subjective and influenced by cultural conditioning.

TONIC

The tonic note or keynote is the central note on which the unit of music is based. So if we sing a melody in the key of C, then the tonic note is C, and the chords in the harmony will only contain notes belonging to the key of C. Usually the note C will sound as the lowest note in those chords, but not necessarily.

TRIAD

A triad is a set of three notes comprising the root (or tonic) and the the third and the fifth notes of the scale. Each note of the triad is separated by an interval of a third.

Triads have different qualities according to the type of thirds that are 'stacked up': a **major third** has four semitone steps between the bottom and top notes, while a **minor third** has three.

▶ A **major triad** consists of a minor third on top of a major third.

▶ A **minor triad** is a major third on top of a minor third.

▶ A **diminished triad** consists of a minor third on top of a minor third.

▶ An **augmented triad** consists of a major third on top of a major third.

UNISON

When two or more players sing or play notes which are the same pitch, they are playing in unison. Melodic lines are sometimes doubled by several instruments at the same time, known as **unison doubling**.

DYNAMICS

The dynamics of a sound covers its volume, intensity and loudness. Full control and use of the dynamic range of an instrument or voice is an important aspect of musical performance. Performances that exist in only a narrow part of the range lack contrast and the listener can lose interest.

FUNDAMENTAL NOTE OR TONE

See overtones.

HARMONY

From a physics perspective, when vibrations are occurring at the same or related rates, they are said to be in harmony. Apparently two pendulum clocks hanging side by side will eventually become synchronised, as it is easier for them to work in harmony. Harmony in music is very subjective. It is the result of any group of tones sounding simultaneously, and can be pleasing or not to the listener. Harmony is the foundation and support for melody.

MELODY

A musical note of a certain frequency is a tone. When the tones 'move about', they form a melody. That is, a melody is a sequence of tones in a composition. Like line drawings, melodies have shape and contour. They can form smooth, curvy lines, stepped, jagged lines, angular shapes or any combination in between. Melodies can exist in any register, but they are usually in the upper register, floating above the harmony.

METRE

Metre is the organisation or arrangement of pulses into groups. The most common metre is four. Most pop music is organised in groups of four beats. Any metre can be used in organising sounds, although Western music tends to favour even-numbered groupings.

▶ When all the players in an ensemble are thinking of the same metre at the same time, I call that **unified metre**. That's how an orchestra plays, with the metre visually represented by the conductor for the players to follow (see the diagram on page 91).

▶ If musicians are playing in different metres I call that **independent metre**. To find this in music is rare, but it is a useful workshop tool for exploring pulse, rhythm and metre.

NOISE

If you like it, it's music; if you don't, it's noise. Noise is what we don't want to hear. We filter noise out of performance spaces with thick walls and doors. We grow accustomed to environmental noise like fridges, traffic, air-conditioners and computer fans, and we don't notice them until they stop. We are aware of the absence of noise in quiet places in the country. All listeners have their own criteria for deciding what is music and what is noise—it's a great question for discussion.

A look at the soundwave of a musical tone, such as the sound of a wind or string instrument, will show a smooth undulating curve. A look at the soundwave of a rubbish bin being whacked will show jagged, angular lines. In general, the more angular and jagged the soundwave becomes, the closer a sound gets to being considered a noise; it is also harder to define the note, or pitch, of a noise. You can pick the tone of a flute, but can you sing the note of a handclap?

OVERTONES

The colour green is comprised of a mix of blue and yellow. When we look at green we don't think of two colours mixed, we just see green. Likewise, sounds have component parts. When we hear a sound we are actually hearing a complex mixture of tones. The lowest tone of this mix is called the fundamental tone. An overtone is any tone which is higher in frequency than the fundamental tone.

The distinctive colour, or timbre, of a sound is created by its overtones, and they create the difference between the colours of, say, a French horn and a trumpet, or an oboe and a clarinet, or a xylophone and a marimba. The same note played on all these instruments will sound different primarily because of the mix of overtones in the sounds created by each instrument.

PULSE

Pulse is the underlying, internalised beat which propels music in much the same way as our heartbeat provides the beat that propels life. The speed of this pulse can vary from slow to fast. Performers need to be experiencing the pulse physically and mentally to perform music. They place their sounds in relation to pulse. Audiences also experience the pulse of music and hear sounds in relationship to it. Some rhythmic music, like traditional African music, makes very little sense to the listener if the pulse is not felt or understood.

▶ When all players synchronise their music-making to the same pulse I call this **unified pulse**.

▶ When players listen to their own pulse and do not synchronise their music-making with other players, I call this **independent pulse**; for example, players may use their own heartbeat or breathing as a pulse.

REGISTER

Sounds exist in a range from low to high pitch. What we hear is limited by the range of human hearing; some sounds are higher or lower than the human range, for example, dog whistles. The area or range that a sound occupies is called its register. Human voices come in a wide variety of pitches from low to high but we classify them (from lowest to highest) as bass, tenor, alto and soprano. Choir arrangements are thus known as SATB. Men's voices are generally lower than women's.

Noises which don't have a pure note still exist in a certain register. It is possible to cup the hands and make a variety of clapping sounds from low to high. Non-pitched percussion instruments like wood blocks, cowbells and drums are usually arranged according to their register from high to low in composition and performance.

RHYTHM

Rhythm consists of the placement of sounds in relation to the musical pulse. Sometimes there are several sounds within the span of a single pulse. This is called the **subdivision of the pulse**. The most common sub-divisions are halves and quarters; however any subdivision is possible.

SATB

See register.

TEXTURE AND DENSITY

Texture and density in music are created by the relationship between independent sounds occurring together at any one time in music. A large orchestra has a great range of textures available in combinations from one up to possibly one hundred instruments sounding together. Texture and density need to be considered in relation to register. A dense texture confined to the low register can support a high solo melody in that the contrast enables the melody to be clearly heard. If a dense texture spans low, middle and high registers, it will mask a solo melody which covers low, middle and high registers.